WORKING WITH THE LAW

WORKING
with
THE LAW

by

Raymond Holliwell

 DeVorss Publications
Camarillo, California

Library of Congress Control Number: 2004108269
ISBN: 978-087516-808-1

First DeVorss Publications Edition, 2004
Fourth Printing, 2011

DeVorss & Company, Publisher
P.O. Box 1389
Camarillo CA 93011-1389
w w w . d e v o r s s . c o m

Printed in the United States of America

CONTENTS

This book is lovingly dedicated to all humanity and to you who have shared in any way to make it possible. Your love, helpfulness, support, encouragement, and inspiration are all bound within these covers – to you I am indebted.

INTRODUCTION

We've all experienced it—that smooth, easy flow when everything falls into place, when solutions appear even before any problem becomes evident. Many times in our life, we've seen our needs met, our peace of mind restored, our goals realized. These experiences point to a harmonious way of life we know to be possible. Yet, at other times, life seems to be a battle, and we struggle, lose out, fail, or otherwise go awry in some way. We feel the bottom fall from beneath us and cannot understand why it happened or what to do about it.

If life can move along effortlessly and orderly some of the time, why does it not do so always? When we ponder this question, often in the midst of discouragement and difficulty, we feel that a key or secret seems to be eluding us. We sense there is something to know about life, something that if only we could grasp and apply, would enable us to be free from the all too frequent frustrations and failures that seem inevitably to befall us.

What is that something? According to the author of *Working with the Law*, Dr. Raymond Holliwell, that something is God—or as he prefers to name it, Law. He states in his preface: "I shall call God working in our lives 'Law.' Interpreting the Law in several ways should bring it more clearly into our way of thinking. Then as we strive to work with the Law we are living closer to God, and such living brings a better understanding."

Dr. Holliwell is saying simply that spiritual laws are Truth principles we can learn to understand and to apply and that the natural consequence of applying them is a happy, harmonious, and prosperous life. His main point is that working with (not ignoring or forgetting) spiritual laws leads to success in whatever endeavor or need is concerned. What makes this book especially valuable is Holliwell's languaging. By using the word Law in place of God, he helps to dispel the confusion and distrust that have thwarted spiritual practice for many people.

But Dr. Holliwell's approach is not abstract; plentiful examples of everyday applications of the eleven spiritual laws he identifies make his book highly practical and empowering. Thus, God is explained in terms that readily make sense to us. Even better than that, we learn definite, concrete ways to become a master of our circumstances using our newfound knowledge.

Dr. Holliwell has a highly logical mind and is an inspired teacher. He employs a clear, specific approach to his subject. For these reasons, *Working with the Law* is an excellent resource for group study. Also, retaining the numbered paragraphs, a feature of the original edition, makes this new edition useful for quick reference to key points. It's worth noting as well that minor typographical errors in the original edition have been corrected here. Other than that, the text is unchanged.

A classic guide to becoming the master of our circumstances, *Working with the Law* is a particularly compelling approach to the subject, combining both analysis and inspiration. To have it available in print again is fortunate.

— Kathy Juline, Editor

WORKING WITH THE LAW

PREFACE

STUDENTS FOR MANY YEARS have come to this School asking for a better understanding of God, and desiring knowledge of the best way to get the most out of life. They have heard God spoken of as being afar off, when He is as close to us as the breath we breathe, closer than our hands and feet. They have heard Him spoken of as: Love, Divine Mind, Divine Intelligence, Jehovah, God, Lord, First Cause, Primal Substance, and other names. Being of an analytical mind I, too, have wanted to know the facts of a Truth. If it is a Truth, there are facts to be had, and they can prove themselves, not alone in Spirit but in a very practical way.

(1)

(2)

It is my intention to present these lessons simply, without high-minded words or vague statements that sound pretty and promising. The terms above named are all synonymous. They mean one and the same thing, and I choose to use a simpler name that everyone will understand. I shall call God working in our lives "LAW." Interpreting the Law in several ways should bring it more clearly into our way of thinking. Then as we strive to work with the Law we are living closer to God, and such living brings a better understanding.

(3)

(4)

Preface

(5) As you grow in knowledge and are able to form better opinions, do not hesitate to change your views.

(6) Remember, "The wise man changes his mind; the fool never." There can be no progress without change, no growth without renewal. There must be a constant stream of new thought—better thought and truer thought—to insure progression in life. As soon as you

(7) perceive the better, let go of the old, grasp the new. To continue to hold on to the old and inferior when the new and superior is at hand is to retard growth, and to

(8) this one cause may be traced many of the ills of man.

Proceed to use your thinking faculty and take care

(9) that it does not use you. Master your mind and guide it intelligently; that is, exercise discrimination in all your thinking. Learn to think as you ought to think, give your mental life to the matters that are absolutely

(10) essential to your welfare, and the balance of your thought to themes of beauty, truth and progress. In other words, live with the ideal, but do not neglect the

(11) practical. Aim to adjust the two, and to strive to be on the outside what you idealize on the inside. Your thoughts make you; and your ideals, principles, or ruling desires will determine your destiny.

(12) Learn to use your powers unless you wish to be used by them. Make a daily effort to use the knowledge you have gained. Try to improve upon all your opinions. Endeavor to obtain a truer and larger conception of each of your personal views. This

(13) process entails effort, but all such mental discipline is highly constructive. It leads to a steady increase of

Preface

mind-power, and it is the mind that matters most among life's actualities. You may occasionally blunder. We are all inclined to do this, more so in the earlier stages of our mental development. However, we learn by our mistakes. Then by the constant use of our intelligence we cause our faculties to grow so strong and alert that in time, we are able to avoid further errors. (14)

Man's problems are mental in nature; they have no existence outside of themselves, and it has been discovered that nearly all will yield up their solutions when subjected to a broad and exact analysis. You can acquire this ability by studying the Law of life and its modes of expression. Then by constant effort use your thinking faculty in constructive ways as you work with these Laws. Have good and sound reasons for all the views you hold. As you try to find these, many of your old-time views will fall to pieces. Form clear and definite ideas regarding your convictions as to why you do as you do, and as to why you think as you think. Such practice is like conducting a mental house cleaning. The practice of clear thinking tends to clarify the mind, tones up the faculties, sharpens the perceptions, and gives one a stronger and better grasp of the basic essentials for a larger and richer life. (15) (16) (17) (18) (19)

Clear and exact thinking is a very great necessity. It is, in fact, a sure means to advancement on the material as well as on the spiritual planes. A line of distinction, however, should be drawn between mere surface thought, that is, ordinary, trivial and commonplace (20) thinking, and real thought, which is associated with the understanding of Truth. The latter is deep thinking which arouses dormant powers, quickens the perceptions, and leads to the enlargement of the understanding. The former is but a passing phase of mental activity, while the latter governs the life of man.

(21)   The shallow, surface thought that we give to the ordinary duties and small things of daily life is not the thought that reforms our character, develops our mind or changes our destiny. It is the positive, deep, and penetrating thought that comes from profound and strong conviction born of a higher perception and a clearer realization of the Truth. The surface idea is not the real thought. The inner convictions which control one's aims, desires, and motives, constitute the real thought of the individual and wholly determine the course of his life and personal destiny.

(22)

Psychologists tell us that every individual is controlled by his convictions, whether he is aware of it or not. Such convictions largely determine the nature of his thinking; the inner thought coming from the heart represents the real motives and desires. These are the causes of action. If his ideas or convictions are wholesome and true to his higher nature all will be well, and he will reflect something of the harmony and beauty and utility of his constructive and superior views in his personal life. If his convictions or ideas are not wholesome and true, he will reflect something that is discordant, inharmonious, and evil.

(23)

Always make it a point of moving forward in your mind, ever seeking to unfold your power of thought and to develop hidden possibilities. Learn to train the mind to clear and exact thinking. Your ability to do so will grow rapidly by regular exercise and discipline. No normal person wants to decrease in power and ability. Therefore, strive to cultivate your intelligence and to express better, bigger, and superior thought on all matters about which you may think. There is so much good in the world that it can outbalance the evil; therefore, you can go on thinking more constructive and good thoughts every day, about yourself, your fellow-man, life, and all natural things, to the constant enrichment of your mind and the improvement of your whole being. (24)

You cannot get the most out of these lessons by reading them once or twice. They should be read often and studied with scrutiny. You will find with each reading something clearer than before.

THE AUTHOR

I

WORKING THE LAW

*"The Lord God made the earth and
the heavens and every plant of the
field before it was in the earth, and
every herb of the field before it grew."*
Gen. 2:4-5

THE QUESTION UPPERMOST in the world of thought today
is whether a man has the capacity, equipment, and
power to control his life; whether he can be what he
wants to be; or whether he is a drop in the great ocean
of life. Millions are affected by unemployment, poverty, and want. Can they help it? Where we have thousands of homes broken on the rocks of matrimony, can
such a breach be repaired? Millions complain of sickness and disorder in countless forms. All this gives
rise to the belief that we are victims of circumstance
over which we have no control. Such belief makes of
us fatalists and karmic addicts instead of masters and
controllers of our destinies. A fatalistic belief is conta-
gious, and when man submits to its influence, believing that the circumstances around him are stronger
than the power within him, that man is defeated
before the race is run.

In the history of the race and the biography of
man, there is a long list of evidences of man overcom-
ing circumstances and meeting his problems of life.

(25)

(26)

(27)

(28)

(29)

13

Evolution and anthropology alike furnish the truth that man is responsible for what he is. He has power to control his circumstances, and by using this power he has created other circumstances more necessary in (30) his upward climb. Yet some, not sure that we create our circumstances, are rather prone to think that they are caused by heredity, karma, environment, or numerous other external things. These are the real reasons, they think, for our failures. They believe in (31) the natural limitations of life; they live in the conviction that as we are, so we must remain; they are sure that what is to be will be.

The scientist on the other hand, searching into the mysteries of human life, reveals to us a wonderful world of power, possibility, and promise. He tells us (32) that the mind is the creative cause of all that transpires in the life of man, that the personal conditions are the results of man's action, that all the actions of man are the direct outcome of his ideas, that we never make a move of any kind until we first form some image or plan in the mind. These plans or ideas are powerful, (33) potent; they are the causes — good, bad, or indifferent, of the following effects, which in turn correspond to their natures. He tells us that these ideas liberate a tremendous energy. Hence, when we learn to employ our minds constructively, we use correctly these hidden powers, forces, and faculties. This, the scientist tells us, is the key to success in living life.

There is a marvelous inner world that exists within man, and the revelation of such a world enables man do, to attain, and to achieve anything he desires

14

within the bounds or limits of Nature. I believe the reason
the famous English literary genius, William Shakespeare,   (34)
is the leading dramatist of the world lies in this realm. The
great Greek dramatists with their noted insight always
saw the causes in some external fate or destiny that
brought about the downfall of their characters, but
Shakespeare saw something within the man as the cause
of his failure or success.

"THE FAULT, DEAR BRUTUS, IS NOT IN OUR
STARS BUT IN OURSELVES THAT WE ARE UNDERLINGS."

We see Hamlet wrestling with his reluctant,
indecisive soul. Macbeth is being pulled and driven by
his ambition. Othello is torn and discomfited by his   (35)
jealousy. Always the characters were battling with
their inner selves as though the dramatist were saying:
"You are the master of your circumstance; call forth
your power, initiative, and ingenuity, and be the
master. Fate is in your hands, determine it." If every
man has the power and privilege to determine his fortune, what is that power? How can we recognize it?   (36)

If all conditions are the result of our actions, and
all actions are the outcome or the fruit of our ideas,
then our ideas must determine the conditions in our
daily lives. An idea is a thought or a group of
thoughts. An idea is an image or a picture in the mind.
There must have been an idea, a mental picture, back
of every well known achievement and invention.
From the beginning this is the creative plan. We read   (37)

15

in the first book of the Bible that the Great Architect, God, saw a finished pattern or idea before it grew. There was a mental picture established within the mind of the Creator before it became a reality on the without in some form of a creature.

> "THE LORD GOD MADE THE EARTH AND THE HEAVENS AND EVERY PLANT OF THE FIELD *BEFORE* IT WAS IN THE EARTH, AND EVERY HERB OF THE FIELD *BEFORE* IT GREW."

(38) Every architect and builder follows the same plan whether he is building or planning a house, a bridge, an institution, or his own life. Every man is his own designer and builder; like the Creator, he makes his creations within before they materialize on the outside. All fears of sickness, poverty, and old age, are (39) impressions, ideas, and mental pictures, long before they become painful realities. Every idea and mental picture must produce after its own kind whether the picture is good or bad; the Law determines it so. The (40) Law does not question or challenge the kind of picture we give to it. It only knows that it must take what is offered or planted, and then proceed to materialize it into a visible form. Some men can visualize great engineering achievements, yet they do not know that by (41) the same method they can overcome their diseases and despairs and enjoy the health and happiness they long for. Mechanical engineering is the same as mental engineering; they are both dependent wholly upon a creative intelligence. Mental photography, like

mechanical photography, produces exactly what it sees. A picture of a homely, unsightly person never turns out to look like a Beauty Pageant winner; nor does the little, short person look tall and large on a photograph. A picture of black will not be white; **(42)** neither can negative, destroying ideas produce constructive and positive results. If the ideas are negative, they will in turn create negative results.

I knew a woman who once lived in a beautiful home in an exclusive suburban district with every comfort that wealth could supply to make her happy. This home was a large rambling house, facing a beautiful lake, with green terraces sloping to its edge. Flower gardens, perfectly kept, were scattered freely **(43)** along each path throughout the estate. She had many servants to help her, and from observation her life was just about as complete as one might dream about. But, with all this wealth and beauty, the woman was heard to remark to her friends that she hoped the day would come when she would be relieved of the big house and all its problems and could live in a trunk. She wanted a room to herself, for herself, and just large enough to move about without any extra space to dust and to keep clean.

A few years elapsed. Her husband died and left the estate to her. She sold the home at a sacrifice. Her other holdings depreciated so much in value through unwise investments and transfers that she had but a small income left.

She went to live with a sister, and, true to her wish, she now has a small room on the third floor and practically lives in a trunk. Whether she is happier now than before I do not know, but I doubt it. One thing I do know; that is, she gradually led herself to the small room and privations when her consciousness began to grow small and limited. She unconsciously touched the creative principle and supplied it with ideas of smallness and privacy and limitation which materialized within a few years' time.

(44) As we assimilate in mind these ideas or mental pictures, we, knowingly or unknowingly, exercise a power to produce them. This creative process continues working night and day until the idea is completed. We cannot picture thoughts of poverty, failure, disease and doubt, and expect in return to enjoy wealth, success, health, and courage. It just can't be (45) done, any more than the photographer can take a beautiful picture of a homely creature.

This creative principle is summarized in a sentence (46) found in Proverbs. It reads: "As a man thinketh in his heart, so is he." You may have read or heard the statement before. It has been taught and expounded by philosophers of every age. You may have tried to prove the statement by ridding from your memory all negative thoughts, but because it took determined and (47) persistent effort, you wearied. Then you dropped back into the current of old conditions and ideas and, if (48) anything, became worse off than before. Others, hearing the statement, were not impressed, for they could not accept the assertion that all inharmonies of life are the results of their own beliefs, or of their past thinking crystallized into beliefs. They prefer to blame

18

this upon something, or someone else. Even God is (49) given a share of the blame. There are others who believe that in God's good time all things will eventually work out to their satisfaction, but this is not so. (50) These people are planning for a heaven to be gained at some future time, when it is actually a condition and state of mind that can be had now as well as hereafter. (51) In fact, unless it is gained here and now, it can never be had in the future. At some time in a man's life he is forced to reckon with this creative law. There is no alternative. Everyone is governed by the Law, (52) whether he knows it or not. Possibly it is the same idea that some have concerning prayer. They think it is God's fault, will, or desire, when they do not get the (53) answer they seek. They use God as their scapegoat and excuse when their prayers are unanswered, or when they are unable to explain some act of God or of Nature. "God's will be done," is one of the most overworked and least understood statements in our day. Some use the idea as a crutch to lean upon, when in reality it is a powerful bridge over which man may cross the deepest chasms and mysteries. It is man's failure, if his prayers are unanswered. The creative Law is ever ready to answer and cannot fail to respond when approached rightly and wisely. At the moment that man is able to contact and to realize the (54) Law, he will at once enjoy the benefits. It is the realization of the Law in action that determines manifestation.

An electrician, for example, does not pray and wait for the electric energy to make up its mind to serve him. He learns first hand the laws of conduction

(55) and transmission in order to know how to cooperate with the law that governs electric energy. After gaining this knowledge he can go ahead and set up the machinery which provides the means to generate and direct the power. Then he can snap on a switch and operate giant machines, create heat, set in motion countless other devices, or flood a room with light. He can do this, not once or twice, but as many times as he chooses, so long as he does not disturb the mechanics or violate the law governing the energy. The same principle holds true in all other sciences, including the science of mind.

There is a scientific way of thinking about everything, a true and a right way that prevents the

(56) needless waste of mental energy and produces the desired results on all occasions. As explained, all things and events, all experiences and conditions of life, are results. All results, however, will vary in quality and in quantity in accordance with the degree of knowledge possessed and in the measure of the mind's activity.

The quality of the results produced by the individual thinker may be good, bad, or indifferent, as may be

(57) determined by conscious direction and choice, or lack of such; some results being harmonious and favorable, while others are discordant and unfavorable, or there may be a medley of the whole. It is absolutely essential to give intelligent direction to the creative powers of the mind to obtain the best and largest results in our particular sphere of active expression. In fact, it is highly important, from the standpoint of use-fulness and common duty, that we should endeavor to (58) understand the mind and its workings, and learn how to cultivate and develop those processes of thinking that will give us mastery over life and its conditions.

Thinking is a perpetual process. It is a creative function of life that is ever going on. We are engaged (59) in it and are producing results of some kind every hour and day that we live, registering within ourselves the exact effects of all our thinking. While we cannot stop thinking, yet we possess the supreme privilege of being able to determine the sort of results (60) it is desired to experience by regulating the form and quality of our thought. How this is done in a simple and effective manner is explained throughout these lessons. Our main object is to arouse the individual to (61) think for himself, to cultivate his own powers, and thereby to take the sure path of self-development and true culture.

The great, self-evident fact, which cannot be too often repeated, is that when we change our thinking for the better, we automatically change our lives for (62) the better. Modern psychology has conclusively demonstrated that a change of thought must precede every change in the life and in the affairs of man.

In the course of our studies we have discovered that the more a mind is undeveloped, the more mate-rialistic or lower its individual point of view; while the (63) more developed the mind, the higher its individual point of view. It does not follow that, because a person is worldly-wise and has retained a large number of

Working the Law

(64) facts and experiences, such a one has a well developed or highly evolved mind. On the contrary, that person may have an undeveloped mind and be largely dominated by the lower instincts. Narrowness of thought, limited views, prejudiced convictions, and (65) materialistic opinions are signs of a lack of real development. Breadth of thought, wide and tolerant views, wholesome convictions, and expanding (66) conceptions are signs of growth.

The small mind, however, need not remain small or undeveloped. It can grow and expand and ultimately become great. The path is clear and simple. (67) Let such a one form his own clear conceptions and strong convictions from the loftiest point of view he can reach, and then proceed to think and act accordingly. Advancement will follow as a natural sequence. The law is that the mind is no greater than its conceptions. As you improve and enlarge your (68) ideas and mental pictures, you improve and enlarge your mind. As you aspire to realize the larger truth, you must inevitably grow in understanding. Again, the greater your power of mind, the better you will be able to conduct the affairs of life to use and advantage.

Next we may ask, if there is such a law of mind, what is the Law's intention? Some may think that the (69) Universal Mind has no intention because It is impersonal. Yet Jesus tells us that the Universal Mind has definite intentions. He says: "Fear not, little flock, it is your Father's good pleasure to give you the kingdom." Thus we see that the Universal Mind's intention is for the universal good; therefore, our intention must take the same direction, knowing that whatever works for the universal good will work for the individual good, (70) for the individual's health and happiness, on this same principle. The principle, that which blesses the whole, will bless all its parts.

When our intention becomes reconciled or cooperative with the Universal intention, then we become an expression of that good. This is working with the Law. When man's intention is as God's inten- (71) tion, and not just a mere personal caprice, a force is called into action which gives direction to the undirected mind power. Working with the Law, when we understand it, may become as simple as touching the light button, like the electrician, which, when we do, floods our mentality with illumination and understanding.

We hear much today about cooperation, united effort, merging of forces, and pulling together as a (72) single unit or team. We know the advantage of team work in our games of sport and play. We learn from our games that no grandstand play or individual "show-off" is dependable. It is likewise true with the game of living life. No man can play the game alone. He must conform with the Law, and it is better to cooperate with it than to be used blindly by it. Someone said: "Man with himself as a partner is a fool, (73) but with God (Law) is a majority." Thus, when man is able to combine or direct all his thoughts, ideas, and desires for good, he will be able to bring forth a continued stream of good. (74)

Again referring to the Master, and appreciating all

Working the Law

(75) the good work and miracles He accomplished, we see that He never took personal credit for the results. He knew the Law, and by working with it, was able to perform miracles to the amazement of the unenlightened public. He said: "It is not me, but the Father (Law) in me that doeth the work." Thus all things work together for them that love good (live the Law), because the love of good unites itself with a stream of good, and not because good steps out of its way to show its gratitude.

(76) All failures in life are due to taking sides with the finite around us. All success in life is due to taking sides with the Law within us. Thus working with the Law may be considered the same as taking the Law into our minds and lives as a silent partner. We are then conscious of the source and creator of all power, and realize and receive the many benefits that surround us.

(77) You who are searching and grasping any and every idea that comes along, in the hope that it will be a short-cut method to solve the problems of life, you who condemn and blame every misunderstood person or thing for your failures and defeats, will never find a satisfying life that way. You will find only an existence, and at its best it will be variable and changing. Life with all its attributes of good is something that doesn't just happen to touch a fortunate few. It is something you must create. It is something you must plan, mentally picture, and think about. You, who are seeking love, fortune, happiness and success, must understand that it is not something

you may find; you cannot buy it nor borrow it from another. No one can give it to you; you must create it within yourself. Your desires and ideas are like seeds you plant in the soil, but these are planted in the soil of mind. After planting the thought-seeds you cultivate them, nurture them, and guard them well until the harvest time. Then you will reap all that you have sown, and abundantly. Of course he who has the cleanest and most fertile garden will enjoy the best returns. (78)

We may realize from this lesson that we have the capacity, for we can think, and in our thinking, create desires and ideas. We have the equipment; it comprises the ideas and thought-seeds that we plant in the soil of the mind. We have the power, for the Universal power of mind is endowed within each and every one of us. All that we may ever desire to have and to be is ours for the asking as we correctly apply the Law of life, the Law of Mind. When a circumstance arises we are not to come under it, to submit to it in servitude, but we are to surmount it, to overcome and master it, by exercising the creative law of thinking, and thus grow in wisdom and power. For, as Dr. John Murray so often said, "We are according to our system of ideas." (79) (80) (81)

II

LAW OF THINKING

"As a man thinketh in his heart so is he."
Prov. 23:7

To THE AVERAGE PERSON life is an enigma, a deep
mystery, a complex, incomprehensible problem, or (82)
appears so, but it is very simple if one holds the key.
Mystery is only another name for ignorance; all things
are mysteries when they are not understood, but when (83)
we understand life, it no longer appears mysterious.

Man is a progressive being, a creature of constant
growth, before whom lies an illimitable ocean of
progress to be navigated and conquered only by
development and culture of his inherent powers. (84)
The progress of the individual is largely determined
by his ruling mental state, because the mind is the
basic factor and governing power in the entire life of
man. Attention should be given to the predominant
mental state, for it will regulate the action and direction of all one's forces, faculties and powers, the sum (85)
total of which will inevitably determine many particular experiences and the personal fate.

The ruling state of mind is made up of various
mental attitudes which the individual adopts towards
things, events, and life in general. If his attitudes are (86)
broad in mind, optimistic in tone, and true to life, his
predominant mental state will correspond and exhibit
a highly constructive and progressive tendency. As

(87) almost all the forces of the personality function through the conscious mind in one way or another, and as the daily mental and physical acts are largely controlled by the conscious mind, it is obvious that the leading mental state will determine the direction in which the powers of the individual are to proceed.

(88) If his ruling mental state is upward bound, that is, aspiring, harmonious, and positive, all his forces will be directed into constructive channels; but if his state of mind is downward in tendency, that is, discordant and negative, then almost all his forces will be misdirected.

(89) It is evident, therefore, that of all the factors which regulate the life and experience of man, none perhaps exercise a greater influence than the ruling state of mind. Mental attitudes are the result of ideas, and these have their origin in points of view; therefore, by seeking true and natural points of view, one may

(90) secure the best and most superior ideas, and these in turn will determine the predominating state of mind.

We are prone to believe more than what we see.

(91) The evidences of the senses are the only facts that some accept, but now we shall realize more and more that it is what we believe that determines what we shall see. In other words, believing is seeing. More defeats and failures are due to mental blindness than

(92) to moral deviations. If one lived only by physical sight, his world would be very small. It is said of a bug that its world is only as large as the size of the leaf on which it lives, and many times it does not live long

Law of Thinking

enough to consume the whole leaf. With man, if he lived according to the senses, the largest sense he possessed would be that of sight. Thus our whole world would extend only as far as we could see. **(93)**

If we believed in the testimony of our eyes we would accept many conditions that are not true. For example, if you look down a railroad track you will observe that at a certain distance the two tracks converge at one point. This is not true. Have you ever stood on the boardwalk and watched a ship slowly sink into the sea as it sailed away? That ship wasn't sinking; our eyes tell us falsely. When you are worried over some obstacle or problem, just remind yourself that it may be purely an illusion of the senses, that it may not be true at all, according to the Law. **(94)**

Did you know that you don't even see with your eyes? Your eyes are like a pair of windows; at the back of the window there is a reflector and this reflector, in turn, forms an image of what you see and sets up a wave current. This wave current follows along thin wires called nerves. This relays the image back to the brain. Here at the brain it is referred to the memory center. If the picture is a common one our memory accepts it readily, but if we are looking upon some new picture, some new scene, our memory does not recognize it, and then we must repeat the picture over and over many times until it makes a lasting impression. Therefore, we do not see with our eyes; we see with our mind. **(95)**

Thought is a subtle element; although it is invisible to the physical sight, it is an actual force or substance,

29

as real as electricity, light, heat, water or even stone. We are surrounded by a vast ocean of thought stuff through which our thoughts pass like currents of electricity, or tiny streaks of light or musical waves.

(96) You can flash your thoughts from pole to pole, completely around the world many times in less than a single second. Scientists tell us that thought is compared with the speed of light. They tell us our thoughts travel at the rate of 186,000 miles per second. Our thought travels 930,000 times faster than the sound of our voice. No other force or power in the universe yet known is as great or as quick. It is a proven fact, scientifically, that the mind is a battery of force, the greatest of any known element.

(97) It is an unlimited force; your power to think is inexhaustible, yet there is not one in a thousand who may be fully aware of the possibilities of his thought power. We are mere babes in handling it. As we grow

(98) in understanding and in the right use of thought, we will learn to banish our ills, to establish good in every

(99) form we may desire. It is our power to think that determines our state of living. As one is able to think, he generates a power that travels far and near, and this power sets up a radiation which becomes individual as he determines it. Our thoughts affect our welfare, and often affect others we think of. The kind of thoughts we register on our memories or habitually think attracts the same kind of conditions.

If we take the thought of success and keep it in mind, the thought elements will be attracted, for "like

(100) attracts like." We are mentally drawn to the universal

thought currents of success, and these thought currents of success are existent all around us. We will psychically contact minds who think along the same lines, and later such minds will be brought into our lives. Therefore, successful minded people help success to come to them. That is how successful living is founded.

The Law of mind is in perpetual operation, and it works both ways. Persons who dwell on thoughts of failure or poverty will gravitate toward like conditions; they, in turn, will draw to them people who accept failure and poverty. On the other hand, we can think on positive conditions, on success and plenty, and in the same manner, enjoy full and plenty. What the mind holds within takes its form in the outer world. (101)

Some think that we must deal with two forces; that is, to attract the good we must do away with the bad, but this is not true. For example, if we are cold we do not work with cold and heat alike in order to get warm. We build a fire, and as we gather around that fire we enjoy the heat that is extended from it and become warm. As we build up warmth, the cold disappears, for cold is the absence of heat. To be warm, we give our whole thought to those things which tend to create warmth. We ignore the cold in thinking of heat and bring forth heat. Prosperity and poverty are not two things; they are merely two sides of one and the same thing. They are but one power, rightly or wrongly used. We cannot think of plenty and then worry about the unfavorable conditions that may seem apparent. We think about plenty, and as we think of it, lack, its opposite, will become absorbed or disappear. All our (102) (103)

31

Law of Thinking

(104) thoughts must be directed to that one thing which we desire in order that our desire may be fulfilled. Our method is not manipulating two powers, not dealing with good and evil, right and wrong, prosperity and poverty, but as we follow the Law of Good and dwell upon that which is good we shall bring to pass all good things.

(105) The mind force is creating continually like fertile soil. Nature does not differentiate between the seed of a weed and that of a flower. She produces and causes both seeds to grow. The same energy is used for both, and so it is with the mind. The mind creates either good or bad. Your ideas determine which is to be created.

(106) A farmer who lived in Nebraska and had come from a small farm in Pennsylvania years before, never could adjust himself to using the binder, a machine that cut and bound grain. He had been accustomed to the old hand cradle and tied his grain by hand. Repeatedly he said to his friends: "That binder will get me yet." He was afraid every time he climbed upon its seat. One day while I was there his horses ran away with him and he was thrown over the reel into the machinery. Like Job, his fears came upon him. It took just a few years to bring into reality the fears that he subconsciously had entertained and accepted.

(107) Our fears can do so much to us that we should be most careful what we fear and worry about. Years ago, when the flu epidemic was raging throughout this country and many were dying from the plague, a newspaper published an item of interest. In bold letters the heading read: Do Not Fear The Flu. It was the

caption of an article written by a local doctor who explained that fear was the greatest enemy of mankind, and that it would have a tendency to break down a person's mental resistance and make him more susceptible to the disease. The world is realizing more and more that we dare not entertain in our minds any fear lest it come upon us.

Whatever we think in our minds must grow. Why do you suppose the farmer goes out to weed his garden and works tediously to eliminate every weed? Because he knows that if he does not clean out the weeds they will grow stronger and tougher and choke out his crop. If some condition handicaps us, perhaps a weed that must be plucked out, it is important to know that the condition is the *effect* that we see; it is not the true *cause* that we see. Dig down deep into the mental storehouse and find out what is that cause. If we cannot discern it, there are others who can. Then weed out the cause by replacing it with the right kind of thought. That is, if it is fear, replace it with courage. If it is a disease thought, replace it with a healthy thought. If it is a limited thought, think thoughts of plenty. Force some issue whereby we alter or change the trend of the thought. Then as we replace the thoughts that are as weeds, they will die of their natural selves, for such weeds die from lack of cultivation. (108) (109)

As long as we allow things to seem real to us, we are putting our energy into it. We are nurturing it; we are feeding it; we are keeping it alive; we are putting our faith into that thing, whether we like it or not, and it must naturally grow, for the law of (110) growth is ever working to produce whatever seed we plant.

(111) In my college days I remember how a number of us were taken on a hazing party. It was purely a fraternal affair, so we were to be initiated and branded. When they came to my chum, they told him to peel off his shirt. He was blindfolded and they were going to brand him with the initials of the order. They branded him with hot tallow from a burning candle. Now you know that tallow dropping from a candle would not burn; at least, it never did burn me. But, my chum was so excited and nervous he thought they were really branding his back with a hot iron. After we returned to our rooms in the dormitory, I saw on his back a perfect letter as though it had been burned with a hot iron. Man can impress his thought on formless substance and cause the thing he thinks about to be created. My chum believed he was being burned, and thought it so intently that a welt rose on his flesh which lasted for two days.

(112) Man is constantly thinking. He can change his thought, but he cannot stop thinking. This thinking power flows in and through him like the very air we breathe. Man's problem, then, is to direct his power of thinking into constructive channels of expression. It is a scientific fact that no power can act without producing some kind of an effect, and by merely thinking we are continually producing effects. These effects register and record in daily life.

When our thoughts are aimless and imperfect, we create for ourselves pain and confusion. This is

34

misdirected energy. Now electric energy, when it is (113) misdirected and uncontrolled, develops lightning, a most destructive agent. Yet that same power of lightning can be harnessed to become a most obedient and useful servant for good. The first question in our self-development is, are we controlled by our thoughts, or are we controlling our thoughts? Are we using our (114) thoughts for gains? Are our thoughts using us for a continued loss?

Jesus said: "Seek ye first the Kingdom of Heaven and all things will be added." Heaven is a state of mind. Therefore, heaven is an orderly, disciplined, constructive state of thinking. To gain all things, we (115) must first gain a disciplined, orderly, constructive state of mind. Have you a disciplined mind? Have you any dominating appetite? Are you emotional? Do you vent your feelings through impatience, temper, malice, hate, pride, envy, conceit, lies, dishonesty and the like? Any of the negations as named, if controlling your (116) thoughts, will delay good from coming to you. Anything in life that dominates us, makes us a servant to its dictates. All our weaknesses and our lacks are due to some compelling influence that blinds us and keeps from us what we naturally would receive, if we were free in mind to receive them.

Man, being a creature of Nature, is endowed with (117) the power to overcome all these mistakes, all these evil forces. That power is unfailing in its operation. When used properly, one can master any trial. Nature has no problems she cannot solve; she has no troubles she cannot remove; all her movements are governed by the (118)

35

Law of Order and Discipline. Man can say and do the same if he will pattern after Nature.

(119) But first note, Nature takes no chances. There are no "ifs" and "ands" or "buts"; her forces operate under a law. If a stone is thrown up into the air, it falls back to the ground again. The Law says so. Thoughts in our minds are governed by a law with the same exactness. Mind is the source and cause of conditions in our lives; hence, it is here that we start to adjust and discipline our thoughts in order to stabilize our affairs. The fact that every problem is mental is another reason why we must learn to control our thoughts to determine our lives.

(120) But is our problem mental? Let us see. If we desire to gain wealth, we find that it is not a place, nor an environment. If so, all the people in one city would be rich, and the people in another city would be poor. Wealth is not the result of saving or of thrift. Many penurious people are poor; many free spenders are rich. Wealth is not due to any certain business, for men in the same business are poor and rich alike. It is something within the mind of man that makes the wealth, and that something in the mind of man is the quality and type of thoughts he entertains.

(121) Look at Nature again. We see she has every movement well organized. A cut flower soon wilts and dies because it has been taken away from the source of its life. If a dog jumps off a barn roof, he lands with a thud and suffers pain for his act.

Instinct warns a dog not to take advantage of Nature. Does the hungry lion in the jungle roar and

Law of Thinking

lash in an effort to find his prey? Instinct warns the lion to be quiet, to steal carefully upon his prey, to stalk his meal. Have you ever observed how Mrs. Cat will patiently wait for hours for Mr. Mouse? These are samples of organized action that is instinctive in any animal. This instinct must be adhered to by man. This is the organized method, the constructive method. A disorganized method would be destructive and negative.

Man must stalk success or any worthwhile enterprise similar to the lion who stalks his meal. Man must work himself up to gain success; he does not fall into it. Just to roar or to shout his statements is not enough. (122) Birds of dollars will not fall out of trees through fright, they will more likely fly away. When our ideas are organized, they are under our control. That is, our thoughts are so arranged that they work together as a single unit. Our minds must be controlled in their expressions so that every process of thought will be in an orderly fashion.

All action is the result of thought. It determines the conditions of life, and to have better conditions in life (123) we must first make efforts to organize our thoughts. We wish to gain the best in life, but we do not know how to think correctly. The average person thinks at random; he has no clear design in his mind to which he can frame his thoughts. If he has a design, he does not direct his daily efforts toward it. Most of his thinking is beyond control, chaotic, and unorganized. This is why disappointment and failure are always near, for they thrive on indecision.

Law of Thinking

(124) We attract only what we think or create; this is the Law of Thinking. To achieve success we must think it, we must work it, we must become it. To advance, we must make some effort to rise. To obtain happiness we (125) must adapt our lives to the Law of Harmony and Order. To rise above any limitation we must organize our thinking along constructive lines. If a man wishes to climb a hill, he doesn't sit down at the base of it and pray to the good Lord to lift him, hoping the Lord will (126) pick him up bodily and carry him to the top, or give him a pair of wings to fly. The natural thing he does is, first to organize his thought; he decides he is going to climb the hill, and then he starts to climb. He climbs steadily, keeping his eye ever on the top. He may find another picking out a better trail; he may wind around; he may slip back a step or two; he may even fall; he may have to stop to rest to regain his strength; but as he keeps his thoughts collected and his desire intent upon reaching the top, he will eventually get there.

(127) A woman wanted to dispose of her home. She couldn't understand what was delaying her answer, for she had been praying, she said, for some time. I asked her, "What do you do towards working with the Law? Tell me what you did yesterday." Well, first she prepared breakfast for her family. Then she got the children off to school. Then, she said, she always spent thirty minutes with her silence and her reading. After that, Mrs. Jones called her on the phone and they had a lengthy chat, but it was of little importance. Then it was time to prepare lunch. After lunch her neighbor called her out to see the garden, and she stood and

Law of Thinking

talked over the fence for more than an hour. "But," I asked, "What did you do in between these incidents?" "Oh," she replied, "whatever came to my notice that had to be done. I was busy all the time, but somehow," she added, "I have never liked housework." Where did she fail? (128)

First of all, she lacked discipline in her mind except where others demanded it. Her husband demanded it, the school demanded it, so she got the breakfast and the children off to school on time. "You didn't make any effort towards selling your house," I stated. "You thought thirty minutes' silence would do it. Instead of organizing your time and work you did just whatever came along." Her housework controlled her; she did not control her time or her work. She saw the truth. She went back home, and each day thereafter outlined her work mentally. If she talked with a friend or neighbor, it was for just a definite time, not any length of time. Each day her work was planned so that she would accomplish something toward preparing to sell the house. Several weeks later a letter came to me in which this woman stated that the house had been sold at a good price, and she added, "Do you know, I really love my work now. When the day is done I have accomplished so much more, and I am not nearly as tired as before. I am teaching my children to be orderly thinkers."

Do you do just whatever comes along? Do you plan your day that something definite will be accom- (129) plished towards your aim, your ambition? One type of people we call "drifters," the latter type we call

(130) "builders." A president of an automobile company whose output of cars was 76,000 last year, put out more than a million and a half. How did he do it? Each day he carefully planned the work so that steadily his organization was becoming more disciplined and cooperative until they worked as a single unit. He said, when interviewed, he planned more than the job required so he was always assured of reaching his goal. Whether he knew it or not, he was in tune with the Law of Orderly Thinking.

(131) If we have any problems, it is because we are not controlling our ideas. Nature has no problems because she is orderly and disciplined. Self-control consists of an organized thought direction; that is, we start out with a well defined aim or objective, think toward it continuously, not just for thirty minutes, plan our time and work so that we are working steadily toward the goal. We fill our day so full of constructive duties that there is no room for idle chatter or waste of any kind to enter in. This development will enable us to move steadily upward toward success. When all things are in harmony and order, problems will cease to be perplexities, and mysteries will cease to be mysterious.

(132) Knowledge and understanding will supplant fear and ignorance, and that which was invisible will become visible, that which was unknown will become known. Life with its circumstances is no longer an enigma, but a clear interpretation of the Law of Thinking. We are what we are according to our state of thinking. We attract only what we think or create.

THOUGHTS ARE THINGS

(133)

I hold it true that thoughts are things;
    They're endowed with bodies and breath and
        wings:
And that we send them forth to fill
    The world with good results, or ill.
That which we call our secret thought
    Speeds forth to earth's remotest spot,
Leaving its blessings or its woes
    Like tracks behind it as it goes.

We build our future, thought by thought,
    For good or ill, yet know it not.
Yet so the universe was wrought.
    Thought is another name for fate;
Choose then thy destiny and wait,
    For love brings love and hate brings hate.

—Henry Van Dyke

41

III

LAW OF SUPPLY

*"Ask, and it shall be given you; seek,
and ye shall find; knock, and it shall be
opened unto you."*

Matt. 7:7

MAN IS NEVER SATISFIED. This fact is deplored by many, but God did not intend that man should be forever satisfied. (134)

The law of his being is perpetual increase, progress, and growth; so, when one good is realized, another desire for a greater good will develop; and when a higher state is reached, another and more glorious state will unfold his vision and urge him on and on. Hence, the advancing life is the true life, the life that God intended man to live. The law of good is universal; for, are we not all seeking Good in some form or another? Science and logic alike declare that the universe is filled with the essential substance of every imaginable good that man can image, and that he is entitled to a full and ever increasing supply of any and every good he may need or desire. We believe, therefore, that it is right and good for man to seek to gratify all pure desires and ambitions. (135) (136) (137) (138)

Here is the key to the law as Jesus gave it: "What things soever ye desire, when ye pray, believe that ye receive them and ye shall have them." Every person, consciously or unconsciously, is operating this law in one or more of its phases. It works universally and on every plane of life's expression. We are all daily draw- (139) (140)

43

(141) ing into our lives the things we most desire and expect, and whether we attract good things or bad things, the principle operated is the same. But as we want more of the good things in life and less of the bad, it will be necessary to understand the law more perfectly, and so be able to adapt our thinking to it in a more direct fashion. Thus we secure the greater benefits that accrue from a conscious, intelligent use of its power.

(142) We affirm repeatedly that God is our supply, and if we would think a moment and trace our supply back to its source, we would agree that the statement is true. The difficulty with some is that they can more easily look to creature for the source of their substance than to the Creator. We don't REALLY believe that God is the source of our substance. We try to think it true, and may theoretically accept it, yet there is an uncer-

(143) tainty. It is hard for some to believe in something they do not see. It is so much easier to believe in what we see. Now if we can see plenty all about us, we are willing to believe it and enjoy it. But later, as we are able to believe in the abundance of good, we shall then see it and enjoy it. Thus at the outset the question is,

(144) which comes first, *seeing*, or *believing*? As we study the facts we shall learn that the latter comes first, and the law is founded on our belief, which in turn determines our sight.

(145) People at one time believed in magic. Once they thought material things could appear right out of the air from nothing and from nowhere. They also believed that things could be made to disappear into

44

nothing. Science has long since refuted this idea and proven such magic to be impossible, except when it is done through some trick in chemistry, a sleight of hand, or an optical illusion. NOTHING can ever become SOMETHING, nor can SOMETHING ever become NOTHING. Substance can be converted, transmuted, and changed in a million ways, but it can never be destroyed.

For example, if we plant an acorn in the soil, it will (146) sprout forth a tree. Each year the tree will bring forth leaves in the spring and shed them in the fall. The leaves drop to earth and become a part of the fertile soil. The tree lives for a hundred years, dies, falls to the earth, and decays. This decomposed timber slowly becomes part of the earth and is hardened into peat and coal. The coal is mined and brought into the home as fuel. Here it is consumed with fire and burned into ashes, and the heat units thrown off are used to warm the home. The ashes are again cast upon the earth, supplying food to the soil, which finally nurtures another seed and causes it to sprout forth and become in time another great tree.

Following the cycle of the substance of a tree, we find it changing form many times; we see it giving off gases, heat units, chemicals of many kinds, and yet (147) if it were possible to be measured accurately, we would find that not one tiny part has been lost. All the supply there ever was, still is, and ever shall be, for nothing can ever be wasted or lost. There can never be a shortage in supply.

Because some people do not see an abundance around them and do not enjoy plenty is evidence that (148) they do not understand or do not apply the Law. In their blindness they say that plenty does not exist, and so far as they can see, they may be right. But when they learn to see with their mind's eye, they will realize differently.

(149) There is a phase of the Law known as DEMAND and SUPPLY which is found in every department of life. Years ago Thomas Edison resorted to its use when he invented the first electric light. When his carbon lamp was brought to the people as a new kind of lighting, far superior to any method then known, did they readily accept it? Many thought it ridiculous and too expensive. They were using candles, oil lamps, and a small percentage of gas lamps. Such light was plenty good enough. Hence, quite some time elapsed before the public was educated to the advantages of electricity over the old ways of light, heat, and power. Not until the people were convinced of the advantages of this new power did they invest in its future, build power houses, set up poles, and string wires all over the town to factories and homes.

(150) How was all this accomplished? When there was a demand for the need of electric power, the supply was forthcoming. Where did it all come from? Out of the earth, out of the air, from water power, steam power, gas, oil, and a thousand and one other sources. It comes directly from Nature, whose foresight created these materials in the earth.

(151) Once our forefathers were in style when they rode the stage, a hack, or a carriage. It has not been so long since one was the talk of the town if he owned a fast

team of horses and a rubber-tired victoria or gig. Where are they now? Gone and almost forgotten. The automobile has supplanted them. How did it all happen? When people demanded a means of traveling with more speed, greater comfort and luxury, necessity gave man an idea. He thought of building a horseless carriage. He worked on the plan, slowly developed it, and slowly educated the public to accept the modern mode of transportation. One outstanding man dreamed of the world rolling on wheels and set out to build a car that the poor man could afford. Today the automobile has become such an important factor in man's life that we wonder how he could have ever progressed without it. You see, whenever man has needed a certain thing in life, an idea has been first given him in mind. He was inspired to develop the idea and then materialize it by converting a piece of mud or metal into a usable form.

Why did people live so long content with the horse and carriage and not enjoy the automobile? Because (152) they could not imagine it. Their minds were not trained to demand such a thing. Was the supply available to build such a machine? There was as much supply at hand then as now, in fact the supply has always been there since the beginning. Thus, it was not God's fault that the auto was so late in coming to man's need. It was man's fault because he had been so long realizing the need. Where there is no demand, there will be no evidence of supply. Our parents who (153) had a horse and buggy consciousness could not attract the new mode of travel until they were able to enlarge their minds to conceive the necessity of the automobile.

(154) The secret of the Law lies in one's consciousness. A man's life consists not in the abundance of the things he possesses, but in the consciousness of that which he has. Man possesses the whole world and all its wealth, yet is only able to enjoy what his consciousness permits him to discern. Somewhere I read a story of a man who lived outside of Pittsburgh and operated a small farm and dairy. Day in and day out he worked (155) laboriously to earn a meager living for himself and his family. One day several men who had been surveying some adjacent land walked across his pasture land. When they were crossing a stream of water that ran through the field, the farmer noticed them stopping, stooping down, and studying the slime and scum that had collected against the crude footbridge he had laid there. One man had scooped up some water in his hand and apparently drank it. Another collected some water in a canteen he carried attached to a buckle on his belt. The farmer was puzzled and wondered why anyone should be interested in that stuff; even the cattle had no taste for it, for they pushed the scum aside to drink the clear water.

Some weeks later a man called and offered him a fabulous price for the farm. Why, the man must be crazy, he thought, he could never get his investment back by farming that ground -- had he not tried it for years. He was joyful at the prospects of getting such value, and readily sold the farm. He moved to Canada to be near his brother and bought another farm. It

wasn't long, however, until some queer contraptions (156)
were set up on the field, and word spread like wildfire
that they had found oil. In a few years that farm of less
than one hundred acres produced millions of dollars
in oil for its owners. The farmer remained poor and
worked hard because he knew only how to scratch the
surface and till the soil. Nature had supplied an
abundance for the man, but he could realize only a
scanty portion. He could see the farm only as acres of (157)
stones and dirt. The Law is not at fault because the
man was poor and had to work so hard to earn a
living. Man will ever be poor as long as he demands of
life a meager living and sees in it a struggle, toil,
hardship and limitation.

The thing we dare not do is to fret and worry
about supply or about where our next dollar is coming (158)
from. Fretting and worry tend to restrict and limit the
supply at hand. They tend to close off the outflow of
substance, whether that flow is small or large. Instead
of lifting us out of limitation, instead of improving our
conditions or increasing our supply, they drag us
deeper into the throes of doubt and fear. Instead of
expecting more to follow, we grow tense and anxious,
which increases our fear and brings us less and less.
Instead of tightening up in our thinking, we must (159)
relax and be more expanding. We must educate our
minds to a larger state of thinking. When we can think
and realize more abundance, we shall receive more
abundantly. This does not mean that the engineer is
destined to be rich while the farmer remains poor. (160)
There are poor engineers and rich farmers. It is not the

Law of Supply

vocation that determines riches, but the demands we
make of our vocations that determine riches. As we
are able to think and to realize more abundance out of
what we already have, we shall not only expand our
thinking, but receive more abundantly. This is the
basic principle of the Law.

(161) The magnet was not charged of itself, but had to be
charged with an electric energy by one who
understood the operation. A magnet in the hands of
an untrained man would be little changed, but in the
care of a trained engineer it could become a strong
force of attraction and do a great good. Likewise the
(162) mind magnet of a person can be stimulated to a strong
force of attraction, if it is possible to get help from one
who already has a full understanding of the Law and
can give him a good start. Of course the mind magnet
can be charged with constructive thoughts, but it will
take some time for these to be effective, and the
student who lacks perseverance may too readily
become discouraged before the work is accomplished.
(163) I always advocate that it is better to get a good start
when possible by getting help, rather than to come
over the slower and more arduous path of self-educa-
tion. Then the student, knowing that the Law does
work, will be able to make rapid progress in his
development and practice.

(164) All the poverty in the world arises from a
poverty-consciousness, whether it be collective or
individual. Why do millions suffer lack, and millions
more die yearly in India from starvation? I am told
that many of them have never in a whole lifetime

50

enjoyed a full meal. Surely it is not because Nature has underestimated the need for so great a people. Surely it is not because there is not enough food to go around. It is because the vision of the people has been limited to such poverty.

Ask the farmer about his crops. He will tell you his (165) problem is not scarcity, but oversupply.

Ask the miner, no matter whether he mines for gold, silver, diamonds, coal, or iron, he will tell you that the supply is far greater than the demand. Ask the scientist, and he will tell you there is food aplenty. There is more food in the air yet undiscovered than we can use. There is more power in a single drop of water or in a lump of sugar than man can realize at this moment. The supply is greater than the demand, and the demand is determined by man's own thinking.

The proposition with most of us is that our power of attraction is too weak to meet the demands. Our (166) mind is like a magnet which draws unto itself its own like, type, and kind. A magnet can draw to itself in proportion to its power of magnetism that is generated or collected within itself. Our mental magnet is greatly reduced in strength by our worries and fears, and our inflow of good is slowly closed off. (167) If our mental force becomes too weakened, we may even repel what little good that is trying to reach us. As we can charge a magnet with electric energy to build up its power of magnetism, so can our mind be charged with a mental energy that builds up a power of attraction.

Law of Supply

(168)   Like Nature, we must follow a natural Law. Nature never builds down hill, always up. To receive prosperity, we, like Nature, cannot perform magic or miracles. We cannot make health or happiness or dollars out of nothing. Nature shows us how we can convert much or little of the available substance into a usable material. The available substance is our thought, and we charge our minds with constructive

(169)   thoughts. Like Nature, to accomplish good our thoughts must always be building upward, must be constructive. If, for example, a drone bee in a hive has decided to lie down on its brothers and only do a half job, does Mother Nature agree and find a part time

(170)   work for the special bee? She does not. She impresses the other bees, who are working hard to collect the honey and fill the hive, to send their soldiers after the drone. It is politely marched outside and stung to death. Nature destroys a lazy bee.

(171)   If thoughts enter our minds that are not full strength, are not wholly positive, like Nature, we must comply with the Law and destroy them. We dare not entertain a half-truth or a lazy thought without weakening our power of attraction and reception. Right here is an excellent place for us to begin with an inventory. We should sieve our thoughts carefully to separate the strong thoughts from the drone thoughts.

(172)   The drones must be cast out and destroyed by refusal to accept them any longer. Then we must carefully guard every thought so that another weak one cannot unconsciously or consciously slip through to play destruction with others that are trying to do good.

Law of Supply

A man came to me one day late in the fall and expressed his fears pertaining to his job. He had been employed for many years in a hotel that for the first time had felt the effects of a dull season. It was rumored, he said, that the management was going to close down the house and let out the employees until spring. He said, "I feel these folks know there will be a shut down, they are in the office of the Manager. What do you think I can do about it?" "There is only one thing you can do," I answered. "Go back to your work **(173)** and realize the Law. If the Law determines your supply and position, then no one but the Law can change it for you. If you will realize this and keep it constantly in mind, I shall help you keep the Law at work. If the Law has another position for you, there will be a door open before this one can close. Go back to your work and ignore the rumors. Let the others fear and fret, but don't let yourself come under their thought. To prove your faith or confidence in the Law, prepare to enter another year's business on your books. Get ready to carry on, and expect your work to increase and improve."

He went back and did as he was told. When rumors grew to realities, he held firmly to the thoughts of increased work and business; thus, he was **(174)** retained during the slack times. He was kept in the office to handle the business, and because of the increased work and responsibility placed upon him, he was given an increase in salary. If he had been allowed to entertain the fears and thoughts of loss and lack, he would have suffered with the rest who were

(175) laid off. This is according to the Law, and the Law is no respecter of persons. If he had allowed his thoughts for good to become adulterated with thoughts of lack, he would have weakened his mental magnet. He could not have attracted any more than his mind was able to receive. It matters not how much we pray or how loud we pray, our prayers can only be answered as we work the Law. The Law will serve us in proportion to how well we serve it.

(176) Robert Collier in one of his books tells of an incident that happened in Chicago. A young man while in the elevator of a large business house was asked the question, "What is your religion?" He promptly answered, to the surprise of others, that his religion was "Sears, Roebuck & Company." That young man is one of the executives of the same company today.

(177) Why? He touched the Law of Supply in that he thought solely in terms of his interests. His firm's success was his success. His concerted interest enabled him to become a part of the firm. Today he has a tufted seat, a handsome office, and a fine salary. If your need is supply, then your religion is the same. Like the young man, your single thought must be abundance.

(178) As abundance and supply are one, then to use the Law you must think supply, talk supply, and live supply with every thought. Keep your thoughts so occupied with ideas of plenty that any and all the drone thoughts of lack or loss will be destroyed.

Remember not to confuse money with supply. Money is but one of the numerous means of supply. Money is not the root of evil, but the love of money is.

Law of Supply

If you concentrate upon money alone and use every (179) means to gather it and hoard it, you are forcing the Law to close out other good. If you concentrate on a part and not the whole, you get only a small part. If you concentrate on the whole, you enjoy all its parts. If you love money, use the Law solely to amass riches, you may gain riches, but you will also lose so much more that is good that your life will be quite empty (180) and lonely. I knew a man who determined early in his life to concentrate on accumulating money. He attained his ambition and became an influential power in his town. He confided in a friend before he died, saying, "I did everything I knew to become rich; I gained riches, but I lost the love and companionship of my wife and the joy of being a father to our children. I lost my health and am spending my wealth to regain my health, but somehow it doesn't respond. Yes, I learned how to get rich, but I never learned how to live."

If we love the Law, use the Law to gain supply and use it wisely, we will satisfy every desire. We will (181) learn how to live wholesomely, freely, and wisely, and there will be no losses. Our lives will be as complete as God, the Law, designed them to be.

There may be many of you who are trying to follow the Truth ideas and who have earnestly affirmed and thought statements for supply, but somehow it has only come in small amounts or not at all. This may be largely due to the fact that your (182) senses are yet too strong for your mind to control. You must see first before you can believe. That is, you are so used to seeing just so much supply or money that in spite of your statements, you believe more in what you see than in what you are trying to think. To you it is necessary first to train your senses to come under the control of the thoughts which you know you must think to conform with the Law.

(183) Florence Shinn gives a clear example of this in her book *The Game of Life*. She tells of a man who was seeking a new position, and having a limited amount of money, was debating in his mind whether to buy a new coat or to hold tight to the money in case he was long in getting employment. He was advised to buy the coat, and it was an expensive fur coat. This reduced his bank account considerably, but it increased his confidence and stimulated his faith to such a degree that his prospective employer caught the spirit of it and gave him a splendid job.

(184) The coat served to enable him to feel prosperous, and the venture strengthened his courage and confidence, so the Law proceeded to satisfy the demand. If such a condition arises, wherein one feels better for seeing some evidence of prosperity, then it is wise to do that which makes it easier for the person to draw prosperity to him. Certainly it is not helpful to work for prosperity and see a stack of bills before you or a condition of limitation and squalor around you. It is better to come away from such a sight and go where the view is more in keeping with the desire of the mind. When I desire to work for prosperity for myself (185) or others, I try to stay in an environment where there is plenty and beauty and where the people around me are not in limited straits.

It follows, therefore, that you can steadily draw into your life any and every form of good you may truly desire, as it is the "will" of God that you should enjoy every good that will promote happiness and progress. All desire is an expression of the will, while to expect good is to demand good, so that both are necessary to attract supply. Therefore, seek to adjust your desire with God's plan, the Law, and expect that every good and only good can reach you; then nothing but good can come. (186) (187)

An abundance of all needed good is the natural heritage of every man, woman and child. That is a vital truth. It is wrong for one to dwell in poverty when there is plenty for all. It is wrong for one member of the human family to accumulate vast wealth at the expense of his fellow man; wrong for one to dwell in conditions of war and chaos when peace may prevail; wrong for the strong to take advantage of the weak; wrong to lack in good of any kind that may be essential to promote the welfare and happiness of the individual. (188) (189)

So, whatever falls short of giving satisfaction, harmony, growth, and increase is abnormal. Nature originally intended that the real needs of man should be adequately supplied; not his surface wants, which are often impulses, but the normal specific needs of the individual, which would be abundantly satisfied were man to live in closer harmony with the fundamental law of supply. (190)

Nature is a prolific producer of blessings which she gives freely to mankind, ever producing all things (191)

(192) for a good and useful purpose. Every individual, therefore, has a natural right to a full supply of every good that he can use or enjoy. Owing, however, to the artificial means man has been taught to use and to depend upon for his supply, he has lost sight of the basic truth upon which this lesson is based. At the outset, let us realize that the material world in which we live is a sphere of effects, and that behind these effects is a world of causes. Then recognize that when

(193) you desire any particular effect, it is because that specific "good" is already in existence in the sphere of causes. Then recognize that when you desire any particular effect, this desire is an appearance of an underlying cause.

(194) This is the Principle upon which our definition of the Law of Supply is based; and when you learn how to operate it in the proper manner, you will be able to draw into your life more and more of the good in whatever form you may need or desire. Everywhere in the world is an omnipotent Principle of Good. We touch it in countless ways. Each thought of good is a

(195) seed for the production of good. You are entitled to all the good you can appropriate and use, and the more good you realize and enjoy, the more you live in true accord with the purpose of this everpresent Spirit of Goodness. Learn to understand how to tap the Source of all Supply for there is no limit to the good that may be developed and enjoyed in your life.

(196) In truth, man embodies every law of Nature relating to his highest welfare and orderly growth. He is not, therefore, separated from any good thing he may

need to enhance his happiness or further his progress. But whether he shall lack or possess that which he needs or requires will be largely determined by the use he makes of his present endowment of intelligence and power. The more man grows in true knowledge and the more he uses his powers in constructive ways, the more good he will create in the circle of his expression, in his own little world.

(197)

THE PROMISED LAND

No more shall I look to the far skies for my
  Father's loving aid;
(198)   Since here upon earth His treasure lies, and
  here is His kingdom laid.
No more through the mist of things unknown I'll
  search for the Promised Land;
For time is the footstool of His throne, and I am
  within His hand.

The wealth that is more than finest gold is here,
  if I shall but ask;
And wisdom unguessed and power untold are
  here for every task.
The gates of heaven are before my eyes; their
  key is within my hand;
No more shall I look to the far skies; for here is
  the Promised Land.

—Alva Romanes

IV

LAW OF ATTRACTION

"To desire is to expect — to expect is to achieve."

THE UNDERLYING LAW that regulates supply in the world of effects has two important phases; one is "desire" and the other "expectation." These mental attitudes represent lines of attractive force, the former being the positive phase of the law and the latter the negative phase, which phases must be complied with to obtain the best and greatest results. (199) (200)

The first phase of "desire" embraces a positive process of attraction; that is, when an individual earnestly desires a thing he sets up a line of force that connects him with the invisible side of the good desired. Should he weaken or change in his desire, that particular line of force is disconnected or misses its goal; but if he remains constant in his desire or ambition, the good demanded is sooner or later realized in part or in entirety. The principle involved is that you cannot long or yearn for anything unless it already exists, if not in form, then in substance; and "desire" is the motive power for calling it forth into visible appearance or physical effect. (201) (202)

It is no use to desire a thing unless you expect to get it, either in part or in full. Desire without expectation is idle wishing or dreaming. You simply (203)

(204) waste much valuable mental energy in doing this. Desire will put you in touch with the inner world of causes and connect you by invisible means with the substance of the thing desired; then, continuous expectation is necessary to bring it into a reality in your life. Much like the pull of gravitation in the physical realm, "expectation" is a drawing force of the mind which acts in the invisible realm.

(205) We all know that many persons desire good things which they never expect nor make any real effort to grasp. They start out well and may get halfway, but not any further. When they learn to comply with the (206) other half of the process involved and learn to expect what they desire, most of their dreams or wishes will steadily materialize. Again, we meet people who expect things they do not want, but which often come. (207) This proves that expectation is a powerful attractive force. Never expect a thing you do not want, and never desire a thing you do not expect. When you expect something you do not want, you attract the (208) undesirable, and when you desire a thing that is not expected, you simply dissipate valuable mental force. On the other hand, when you constantly expect that which you persistently desire, your ability to attract (209) becomes irresistible. Desire connects you with the thing desired and expectation draws it into your life. This is the Law.

Should you be oppressed by poverty, hardship, limitation, or lack of any kind, begin now to operate (210) this Law of mind and gradually command more and more of the Good in the form of better things and improved conditions. It is your right to be happy and free. We should seek, therefore, to learn more of the unseen laws of mental creation and the marvelous possibilities dormant within our beings. Nature does not deprive us of any good and desirable thing, but has provided us with the mental equipment and inner power to acquire and enjoy all the essential good to insure a happy and worthwhile existence. (211)

Application is the test of adequacy, as knowledge is of little or no value unless it can be used to practical ends. Here is a simple method in the beginning for using the power of mind to increase the amount of good in our lives in conformity with the Law. Form a clear and well-defined mental picture of what you want. Do not specify its particular form or how it shall come, but simply desire firmly and gently the greatest amount of good in that direction. Avoid a tensed state of mind or any condition of strain or anxiety. It is better to do your mind-picturing in odd moments when in quiet and restful conditions. Let the idea or plan of good unfold into a vivid mental picture, much the same as though it were a moving picture upon a screen. Do not force the thought, as pressure causes congestion and confusion. The calmer and more peaceful you are, the better the results. The main thing is to hold the thought. Then proceed to nourish your desire or want with a calm, confident conviction that what you seek will come. As you persist in this state of mind, the good desired will tend to gravitate towards you. It may come almost at once as in respect to little things of less consequence, like an invitation, a book, (212) (213) (214) or meeting a friend on the street, or it may come by degrees over a period of time, according to the clearness and strength of your demand and the particular form of good desired. In the meantime, be reasonable and practical and do what you can to promote its coming. I have little confidence in the Lord answering the one who rocks in an easy chair and waits for the desired thing to be placed on his lap. Somewhere it says the Lord helps them that help themselves. Yes, action spells results. This supplements your mental creative process and provides the channel for its expression. Then leave the results to the Law. As you do your part, the Law will do the rest. How well or how accurately you cooperate with the Law determines the duration of time apparently required to bring forth your supply. Time is a period created by man; Nature knows no time and always responds in the present, in the now.

(215)

In some instances, results that seem almost magical will appear. Often where there has been a deep, longing desire for a particular good with no expectation of its realization, the addition of "action" will finish the process with the happiest results. In fact, you are always on the right side of the Law when you combine the two essentials of "desire" and "expectation." You operate a hidden intelligence that puts you in touch with the actual ways and means of materializing your desires. The principle underlying this process of attraction is as sound and as demonstrable as any principle in the science of mathematics. We all employ it every day, more or less,

(216)

(217)

but usually unconsciously, and therefore imperfectly.

Finally, do not desire or demand what rightfully belongs to another, in the sense that such a one would suffer by deprivation. Only desire that which will round out your life to make it fuller and happier, and also that which will enable you to help others into better and happier conditions. Aim to be normal in your demands, and use the intelligence with which God has endowed you in discriminating between rational and irrational demands. The innate desire of your being is for Harmony, Satisfaction, and Plenty. These conditions will be obtained more and more in your life as you live in accordance with the Law, and constantly expect a continuous increase of Good as an evidence of your growing faith in the wisdom and all-sufficiency of the great Source of All Good.

(218)

(219)

The mind is a magnet and attracts whatever corresponds to its ruling state. Whatever we image in mind, whatever we expect and think about, will tend to bring into our lives the things and conditions that are in harmony therewith. Science has convincingly proven the existence and constant operation of the Law of mental attraction. For this reason everyone should be doubly careful about how and what he thinks. Our predominant mental attitude is the primary cause of most everything that comes into our lives, and the sooner we realize this truth, the sooner we shall begin to improve our lives and progress.

(220)

(221)

We must seek to become imbued with the desire to advance, and give the Law a chance to help us. Everything will then work toward our aid. Obstacles

(222)

Law of Attraction

will strengthen our resolve to win. Discouragement from others will only serve to strengthen and to arouse us to a stronger activity. We will see more clearly and understand more fully that every difficulty is an opportunity to advance, every stumbling block is a stepping stone to success. Our so-called burdens will lose their heaviness because the

(223) Spirit within us is unconquerable, and when invoked by desire and aspiration will unfailingly come forth in greater power and richer intelligence. This will guide our thoughts and actions into those pathways that lead to the heights of conquest.

The Law of mental attraction acts along the same lines as the law of gravity; it is as definite and as

(224) accurate. You have heard the Law expressed in such statements as "Birds of a feather flock together" or "Like attracts like" or "Things equal to the same thing are equal to each other." The thoughts and the actions of people draw to them people of their own type and kind. It is difficult to tell one just where he may fail to

(225) attract his needs, as no two people think alike and therefore no two people make the same mistakes. However, I shall name and explain the three steps one can use to build up realities. By following closely these suggestions, he can note where he may have failed:

(226) INTEREST — The first step to take is called interest. Interest is paying special attention to some object or thing. It is being definitely concerned about someone or something. Interest is tending to see in the outer world what is already existent in one's mind. Things you think of that give you joy, pleasure, wisdom and

satisfaction are interests. I recall one woman telling me that she invariably could see cripples in a crowd quicker than any one else. They seemed to draw her (227) attention to them and excite her sympathy. It was because she had once been injured and was wheeled about for several months packed in a cast, and the memory of the experience was fresh in her mind and created the interest.

Our interests are largely individual because we do not think alike; one person may find interest in some (228) things that another would fail to see.

Recently my wife and I went out exploring along a dried up river bed on the desert. She was especially (229) interested in collecting bright stones containing gold, silver, copper, and iron that are commonly found in this country. I, in turn, was looking for gourds that I knew would grow wild where there had been mois-ture. I was interested in gathering the kind that the native Indians used in their hogans, and particularly the kind they selected for their ceremonial dances. There we were together, she walking about picking up these rare stones, and I looking around for the vines that held the gourds. I didn't even see the stones, and I am sure she didn't see many of the gourds. Both walking together, yet we were seeing differently because we were looking for different things. We see in life that which interests us the most and pass blindly by that which is of little or no interest. It is here (230) in this simple practice that many of us may be making our mistakes. We may be so interested in things that are not prosperous, joyful, and healthy that we pass by the very things we desire most and overlook the means of our health and prosperity. With our interest so engrossed in seeing the lesser, either through habit or ignorance, we fail to attract the greater things that are all around us.

(231) A young man came to me one day asking what he could do to increase his income—he was dissatisfied with a meager earning. I learned that he was an electrician. His work occupied several hours a day. He liked his home, enjoyed his garden, his newspapers, and occasionally stepped out socially. I thought he was getting well paid for his efforts and told him so. I added that if he wanted more earnings he would need to stimulate his interests and be deserving of it. God feeds the birds and supplies an abundance of food, but He does not put the worms into the bird's **(232)** mouth. The bird must at least go out and search for the food. So it is with all of us; we must do something about it more than wishing or praying.

(233) He decided then that he would increase his capacity as an electrician, so he went to a class at night school and laid aside his newspapers for books and other material. He became interested in radio and was enthusiastic about its possibilities. This interest drew him into new circles and landed him a position with a growing radio company. In a very short time he had found a new pleasure and tripled his meager earnings. No one is to be blamed for the dissatisfied life but the man himself, because he failed to expand his interests with his desires.

It is so easy for people to allow themselves to get **(234)** into a rut, and it is always a mental rut before it becomes a material one. People drift along unknowingly, unconsciously, and aimlessly into unhappiness and blindness. A very lovely person came to me with a problem, the like of which has caused many a woman to give up and lose the very thing she wants most. This woman had a nice home, a well-providing husband, many servants, and two fine sons to be proud of. But, with all that, she was most unhappy. When her boys were growing up she devoted all her **(235)** time to their training and care. Now they had married and were making their own homes. While she was so tied at home her husband was becoming a successful man, and this took him out to his clubs and made new friends of other women as well as men. He was quite occupied with his interests; he came home at nights, but most of his weekends were spent elsewhere. Here she was with a big house and servants, plenty of money, but no love or happiness. She realized the breach was widening, and knowing that soon her husband would want a divorce, she was forced to seek a way out.

After a lengthy analysis, I learned that she had a spark of interest left in art and literature, so recom- **(236)** mended that she take a trip abroad for the summer to see new sights and to plan a busy winter with new studies. She returned feeling refreshed and anxious to begin the work. She joined a literary club and liked it. Gradually she worked into some small dramatic parts until one day her interest burst out into a flaming desire to go further with the work. Home, servants, loneliness, all receded with the new ambition. In short, she advanced into radio work and has been very successful. Her sons are proud of her achievement, her husband has become almost jealous with his attentions, and her happiness is supreme.

(237) You see, one must keep up some interest. One must keep his mind active and keen in order to avoid losing one's attractiveness and satisfaction. Our highest interests should govern our thoughts and not the material things. The material things are only the means through which we express our interests. A strong magnetic power is founded upon a strong idea or principle. This idea or principle directs our interests, and this in turn develops an inner power of attractiveness.

(238) A young woman, whom I know very well and shall always prize as a friend, is not a beautiful girl as far as beauty goes, but she is most attractive. She has a wide circle of friends and verily charms them wherever she goes. When asked one time what it was she possessed that seemed to cast a spell over her admirers, she said, "I can't accredit it to my physique, nor to my brand of cosmetics, but I believe it is because I love frankness, truth and a pure mind."

(239) Innumerable examples can be told of men and women who have attained success and fame because they have loved and lived some principle of good. To live such a principle and to follow it with interest will, according to the Law, always attract good.

ATTENTION — To have a high interest is not enough. (240) We must inject this interest into our daily labors. Our attention must portray our interest, and the keener our interest, the more intense will be our attention. It is our interested attention that draws from the outside world such facts as are formed in the mind. As we direct our attention to our interest, this magnetizes our power of attraction which draws to us much of the same type as our thought. When much of our interest is taken up with our full attention we shall find that most of our petty and selfish leanings will be absorbed by our higher interests and we will steadily progress.

I recall years ago when I was yet a student at the University that I would often pass through the (241) terminal of Williamsport where a certain man had his offices and was then a junior supervisor for the Pennsylvania Railroad. Often it would be after working hours when I passed the building, and frequently it would be late in the evening, yet I would see his office lighted and find that he was busily engaged in finishing up some important work. It seemed that he lost himself in his interest for his work, and all his attention was drawn to benefit his employer. Years passed and the day came when I met that man and knew then why he had been steadily promoted from one position to a better one. Today he is next to vice-president of the largest railroad in the world. Whatever he did, he did it with all his might and main and his attention never waned from a job until he thought it well done. I learned from him that he did not wonder when he would get his next raise in (242) pay or change in position. He just worked, he said, and the advancement came without worrying about it. I believe another young man expressed this Law in action years ago when they thought it was impractical idealism. He said: "For whosoever will save his life will lose it. Whosoever shall compel thee to go a mile, go with him twain." Whosoever will find himself great must render great service. Whosoever will find himself at the top must lose himself at the bottom. The big salaries are paid to those who travel the undemanded extra mile. The man whose attention becomes lost in his interests will grow to worthwhile accomplishments. Emerson said: "See how the mass of men worry themselves into nameless graves, while here and there a great unselfish soul forgets himself into immortality."

(243)

(244)

Yes, you say, I know of men who have had such advantages and opportunities to forge ahead, but they didn't succeed as your friend. They had influence and money and brains, but somehow they did not reach the top. Granted that they had all the material and physical advantages that any average man might need to skyrocket to the pinnacle of success, yet they lacked something within themselves. The source and cause of all successes lies hidden deep within the mind, and one must give one's attention and interest first to principle and then to fact. What do I mean?

(245)

If you believe in honesty, then you support the principle of honesty with all your attention. You direct this attention to do and think all things in an honest manner. If you should have an opportunity to cheat or

(246)

steal from another you adhere to your principle and refuse to take advantage of what may seem a trivial thing. They always seem trivial in the beginning, but that is only the beginning. Such trivials grow with a cancerous rapidity. You rarely see the surface record for remaining loyal to your standard, but in time you will not only see but feel its satisfaction. As you watch closely your dealings and force every issue to comply with your principle, you are charging your mind with honesty and it becomes magnetic to attract honest endeavor and permanent success.

Next, take truth and follow it along until you have (247) worked it the same way. There are so many ways that truth may be challenged that you need not expect to accomplish your work in a week or two. It becomes a growth. After a time you will find your interest and attention so taken up with truth in all its forms that you will no longer attract deceit or dishonesty to you or in your affairs. I remember a statement I heard when I was young in this work. The owner of a store spoke of a little lady who often came in to buy cards (248) and gifts for her family. It had been suggested that she pass off some inferior articles on the little lady, but the woman replied, "Oh, no, she is too honest to be cheated." I wondered then why she had made the remark, but I understand it now. Such can be said of all of us when we earn what that little lady had earned.

A president of an eastern college came into our Chapel one day while Mrs. Holliwell was at the book (249) cases. He said he had read a few of the books that were on display in the window and was especially impressed by one book called *The Game of Life and How to Play It,* by Florence Shinn. He thought the title very attractive and of interest to anyone. "Do you know," he said, "I learned to look upon life as a game, and I started out as a poor boy with few advantages, but I played the game. I did not have the help that so many of these books may offer. I succeeded, and now I am telling thousands of boys and girls how I played the game. I built my success on three common principles—Truth, Honesty and Sobriety. I measured my living with these standards, and I have won a happy life."

(250) Set up a standard or a measurement for yourself if you have not already done so. Take one thing or one thought at a time and build upon it. As you strive to give your attention to some constructive interest, you will cease giving so much attention to a lesser one. You do not have to work over the things as some folks may do. They go about treating against dishonesty and the like when they should adjust their minds to be (251) free from thinking and fearing dishonesty. The Law requires us to make the correction within ourselves, and if we do our work there, it will proceed to work for us outwardly. It is our thought which stimulates interest and directs our attention; therefore, let us not wander away from the source and cause of attracting (252) the things we do not want.

EXPECTATION—The last step we take is expectation. This is an active form of attention; it is attention with intensity. It may be likened to the actions of a cat that waits patiently at the mouse hole. The cat expects to

74

catch its prize at any moment; he expects to get the mouse because he believes he will get it eventually. If **(253)** the cat did not believe and expect to catch the mouse, his interest and attention would lack that intensity which is now present. His energies would not be so actively called forth. When you believe in the probability of success in your undertaking, you experience the keenest interest in your work. This interest is **(254)** intensified with expectation and anticipation. Through this you will draw to you the success you are working for. Your expectation must be built up with your interest and attention.

When the widow came to Elisha and asked his help to meet a problem of finance that meant the freedom or slavery of her two sons who were to be held **(255)** for her husband's debt, Elisha promptly asked her what she had that could be converted into money. She had nothing more than a pot of oil, but that was something, so Elisha told the widow to collect other vessels from her friends and go into her home and there pour out what oil she had. She poured the oil until all the borrowed vessels were filled, and when she had filled the last one, the oil stayed. There was not a drop left over. They followed the routine of our lesson, and as she reached the last vessel and the end of her expectation, she found the supply shut off. She was able to receive only as much oil as she had expected, and her expectation was measured by the number of vessels she had collected. Elisha had set the Law to work, but she had determined how far it would go by her thought of expectancy. She might have hoped for

75

(256) much more, but she got only what was expected. If you are working for success, health, or happiness, you may wish for a lot, but you will only enjoy as much as you are able to expect. If in your heart you doubt or fear that your need will be met only in part or not at all, you can know that you will receive that much and no more. When you pray for one thing and then fear and doubt that you will receive it, you diffuse your mental forces and can attract only what the lesser thoughts believe and expect.

(257) A prominent doctor was asked why it was that he was able at times to reach cases that others had failed to reach. He said: "I never expect a patient to be too far gone not to survive. I fish around in my mind for some idea of what to treat, and sometimes those ideas are very simple or strange, but the moment something inside me clicks, I accept it and use it." He said he had never failed to help a patient when he firmly expected his recovery.

(258) When we charge our thoughts so firmly with the idea that there are no failures, then we expect success. Our mind becomes strengthened with our conviction and, like a magnet, draws to us through the principle upheld whatever desire is uppermost at the time. To desire is to expect, and to expect is to achieve.

V

LAW OF RECEIVING

*"Give and it shall be given unto you,
good measure running over."*
Luke 6:38

UNDERSTANDING REDUCES THE GREATEST to simplicity, and lack of it causes the least to take on the magnitude of complexity. In order to make Christianity practical, we must understand Christianity and obey the law on which it is founded. The teaching of Christ shows the way back from wrong results of selfish living to the love, intelligence and power of God. By a man's words, deeds and actions, he reveals whether he has as yet found the way. God exists in man as man's highest concept of perfection, and comes forth through man's faith and works as a redeeming love, intelligence, and power. (259) (260)

He who seeks the Father, with "getting" as his objective, does not seek Him in trueness of spirit. To the extent and so long as any material object remains between the mind of the seeker and the Law of God the two are held apart and do not become one. In the same degree that a man holds to personal opinion and desire, he is limited in knowing the mind of God in its entirety. (261)

In a state of limited understanding, we reason that we must get before we can give, and then we turn and walk in the same mental rut as before by reasoning that we must give before we can get; but in our lack of (262) understanding, we continue to leave the "getting" idea foremost in our thought and we shut out the spirit of giving.

(263) Giving, which is the first or fundamental law of life, is the first law of all creation. The attitude of getting is the law of life in a congested state, or in repressed action. As long as "getting" dominates a mind, that mind is in a paralyzed condition, being limited in its action in accord with the fundamental law of creation.

(264) The radio has aided greatly in explaining the process of the law of giving and receiving, or prayer and blessing. The principles involved are very similar. In fact, they are the same, except that one is mechanical and the other mental. When the operator projects a program, he stirs up a vibration in the air that goes forth to accomplish what it will. He has nothing more to do with it after it has been projected. The ether, or the air, carries the vibrations to any station that is capable of receiving and reproducing it.

(265) When we pray, we in turn stir up a vibration with our desires. This, also, is received by a force determined according to the power, the purpose, and the sincerity of our prayer. Often when we pray we think that all that is necessary is to keep on praying, with the result that we never adjust ourselves to become receptive to receive our answers, and so complain when we do not get them promptly.

(266) A dreamer or a wisher is one who is continually praying, sending out his ideas, his desires, and is so busy dreaming that he gets all his enjoyment out of his

Law of Receiving

dreams. He doesn't know or realize that to release his dream and allow it to go forth to accomplish what it will, will in time return to him for good. After you form a definite clear outline of your desire, then release your thought God-ward — let it go — like throwing a ball out with no string or rubber attached to bring it back to you. (267)

"Man's extremity is God's opportunity" is true, for when man reaches his limit, he hopelessly stops his efforts. When he relaxes from his strain, the Law has a chance to reply to his desires, and things begin to change for him. Have you not seen this work in trivial things, such as books or clothing or invitations or a desire to see a certain friend! Possibly at some time you sent out a thought or a desire and then forgot completely about it. The next thing you knew, you had that book presented to you; you received the invitation; or you were walking down the street and bumped right into the friend you so desired to meet. Yet, somehow when it comes to more important things, to larger things, we fail to release our desires and prayers as readily, and anxiety and tension hold everything fast. Nothing worthwhile is accomplished. The mind is like a sponge. We squeeze it hard with our anxious thoughts, but not until we can release the pressure and allow the sponge to take its normal shape can it become absorbent and receptive again. (268) (269)

Once we have expressed our needs through prayer or otherwise, some believe that is all we must do. On the contrary, we are working with a law that is definite and active, and this is only the beginning of our work. (270)

Law of Receiving

The principle of life upon which this Law is based is clearly written. It reads, "Give and it shall be given unto you, good measure, pressed down, shaken together, running over." Giving always precedes and predetermines the reception, whether you are giving your thought, your word, your service, or your deed.

(271) Some folks may consider this Law as a two-way law; that is, half the time you should be busy giving and the other half of your time you should be receiving. It is like the proposition of heat and cold; they are two sides to the same law. That is, if we concentrate upon cold and hope and pray to get heat, we are likely to freeze to death. What we must do is to give all our thought and effort toward building a fire or seeking that which will create heat to warm us. If we concentrate upon receiving, not giving any thought or idea or desire to build upon, we, in like manner, may perish.

(272) The Law says, "It is more blessed to give than to receive" and "as you freely give, you freely receive." Unless we are free to extend or give out our desire, our good, the Law will not have any pattern to work with. It cannot proceed to supply any need without a pattern. Many try to work the Law backwards, and for that reason get little or no results. They say to themselves, "Well, after I get, then I will give." If you wish any good thing, you must first give some good to build upon.

(273) A young man gives his girlfriend a gift, a paste diamond. Later when he got into financial difficulties, his friend, most anxious to help him to tide over, wrote a kindly note and wished him every success in meeting

his obligations. She enclosed the gift he had given her and suggested that he sell it to satisfy his need. The young man was sorry then that he had not given his friend a diamond of real worth. He got back at a time when he needed help most, that which he had given out, an imitation instead of the genuine.

When we speak of giving, most people have a tendency to think first of giving their money. Money, an (274) object of human affections so passionate that men will slay and steal to gain its possession, is by nature so obedient to our will that we can hold it gently in our hand or fold it fondly in our purse without feeling any resistance from its nature. With all the selfish getting ideas which man attaches to it, man has not changed its nature or its purpose. What does money get out of constantly giving itself into hands that so eagerly grasp it? Nothing. Nothing beyond the joy of giving itself in the fulfillment of its mission. Man may do some terrible deed to obtain it; he may pay it for something detrimental to his progress; but in all these exchanges man, not money, loses value. Just as the sun shines on the just and the unjust alike, so money passes through the deserving and undeserving hand to accomplish its work. Its purpose is exchange without discrimination. Leaving the latter to the mind that is using it, money goes merrily on its way, losing nothing in self-value, in giving itself.

Money came into form to fill the need for exchange and on that purpose it is "all intent." Let our attitude (275) toward it be what it may, money will remain true to its nature as long as it is needed by its master, Man. If we

Law of Receiving

fail to pay full value in an exchange, we fail to understand the prospering Law back of the idea. Money represents the law of services; its value is the estimation of worth placed upon it by the mind of man, while its form is designed to insure the easiest exchange. When (276) we give our best in some useful service, forgetful of self, concentrating on the joy of giving instead of concentrating on the returns, we find that our purpose and the purpose of money have blended and we come together in righteousness and eternal good.

So often I hear people say, "Well, I do give, and sometimes until it hurts, but I seldom see any sign of a return." There is a right way and a wrong way to give. There is a careless, impulsive giving and there is a care- (277) ful, scientific giving. When we give to a person or group of persons where we are retarding progress, we are wasting our substance. Where we give to one who doesn't put forth the effort to help himself, we need not expect a good return.

Nature does not support a parasite or a loafer, but she gives her energy to the ones who are struggling (278) forward. She lets the parasite and the loafer see that she will help if they put forth the effort to help themselves. But with us, if we support a loafer in what he is in, how can we expect any good returns? Rather the loafer becomes arrogant and demanding for more and more relief, until we wonder where and when it will end.

A woman once gave her daughter, when she married, a home fully furnished, and set the son-in-law in (279) a good business. The business from year to year was always needing more funds to carry it over, and she

continued giving her money to him until it was almost
exhausted. When she had gotten down to a small
income and living in one room, she wanted to know
why she was not blessed for her generosity. She gave
as she thought best, but it paid in losses and bitter
words. The son-in-law demanded more help until she
had no more to give, then she was unwelcome in their
home and invited to leave. Her mistake was in her
judgment. She was as much at fault as the dependent
son, for she was part of the cause of his failure. I directed her to stay away from the young couple and let
them sink or swim by themselves. I was sure they
would find themselves. She followed my advice, and (280)
within a year the young man had put his business on a
paying basis. For the first time it was operating at a
profit. The home life was restored to a normal state,
and all were happier because their efforts were being
directed into right channels. The young man was
proud of his efforts that enabled him to make good on
his own merit. A practical interpretation of the Law is,
when you see someone making an effort to help him- (281)
self, that is the time to assist him, but do not give of
your substance to the one who will not help himself, or
at least try. The latter type will not only misuse your
gift, but will abuse you if and when you cease giving.

Jesus gave his substance always where it would do
the most good. He fed the multitude because they were (282)
seeking good, not because they were begging food.
Nowhere do we find Him giving as much as a thought
to anyone except those who desired to improve and
grow. He cautioned others about unwise giving, "Do

(283)   not throw your pearls before swine lest they trample them under their feet and turn and rend you." He meant simply, do not give your substance to anyone who cannot appreciate it or improve with it. It is as foolish as giving a child a loaded gun and expecting him to realize the danger as you do. Sooner or later the child through lack of appreciation will either hurt someone or get hurt, to the sorrow of all concerned. You cannot build something on nothing and expect something in return. If, in your giving, there is no prin-

(284)   ciple of good in some measure, no matter how small, to add to, then you are casting your pearls away. You are wasting your substance.

Many have found tithing a successful form of giving, but the questioning mind wonders. Why would tithing be more potent than any other form of giving? It is more potent because you touch the Law of Giving

(285)   and Receiving in a definite, orderly, or systematic way of giving. You establish a methodical plan of giving which creates a steady flow of reciprocal good to be received. When one's method of giving is sporadic or occasional, one's reception of good is irregular and uncertain. Scientists analyze it; they say that tithing gives man a self-reliance, a confidence which enables him to build up a positive mental attitude which attracts success. Others say that a tither already has considerable confidence to take the chance to spend his money that way. This makes him a positive type and attracts only positive and goodly conditions. Then there are others who take a spiritual view toward tithing and assume that God is their partner and they

Law of Receiving

are paying only one-tenth of their receipts as His share. Then, too, some make the mistake in tithing when they give for selfish gain or when they make a bargain of it. Remember, it is not the money you give; it is the idea back of the giving that is so vital. If you give money and the idea is wholly one of bargaining, your mind is not free; therefore, your results cannot be free and full flowing. Tithing, no matter what one may think about it, if one thinks at all, has a tendency to bring man into line with the Law of Giving and his results will be in proportion to the honesty, sincerity, and spirit of his gift. (286)

Jesus praised and blessed the widow who gave her all, her mite, into the church coffer, but criticized the rich man offering his bags of gold. Why do you suppose He took exception in this case to praise the lowly gift of the widow? He knew the Law of Giving was in action; it was the spirit of her gift that prompted His blessing. When John D. Rockefeller was a poor boy he was able to apply the Law early in his life. When he earned his first money, he kept a record of his givings and his receivings, and he kept a ledger all through life. It is known that he gave away more than one-half billion dollars. Possibly we can judge why he received so much to give. (287) (288)

But after we give, that is not all we must do. Our next step is to prepare to receive the response or results of our giving and to receive, as the Law states, good measure, pressed down, shaken together, and running over. This is the most interesting part, because our preparation shows our active faith. Instead of rocking and waiting, we are preparing and working. This, in (289) turn, enlarges our view. It stimulates our interest, it disperses our doubt and fear, and energizes our power of reception. This was clearly illustrated by Elijah, the Prophet, when the three kings came to him and asked (290) him to pray for them that they would be victorious in battle, and that they might have rain to supply their soldiers and animals. Elijah told the kings to go back to their camps and prepare for the morrow; prepare to receive the water they asked for by digging ditches. Now, if you have ever been on the desert, you will know that it was a most foolish idea to dig ditches in the sand and expect rain to fall, but the kings did as they were told. They prepared for the rain by digging the ditches, and clouds gathered, and rain fell, and the ditches were filled. The men and their beasts were satisfied; their thirst was quenched; and going into battle strengthened, they were victorious. Elijah, knowing the Law, instructed them to prepare and made the way easy for them to receive.

(291) The key to the Law then is: *we are continually drawing into life what we give and expect.* Whether we attract good or bad, it is governed by this same principle. You have probably made the remark, "Oh, yes, it is just as I expected," and especially when some unpleasant condition or circumstance arose. You invited the condition just because you gave out the thought of expecting it. You can also expect good to appear on the same principle and you can help it to come to pass by the method of your preparation. Many failures in demonstrations (292) are because we do not force our expectations to keep apace with our desires. Very often we desire one thing

Law of Receiving

and expect in our hearts another, which creates confusion. The Master said, "A house divided against itself cannot stand." When a mind is confused, there is no cooperation, nor is there united force to attract the strength it requires. Positive mental radiations will drive away all clouds of doubt and fear with confident (293) expectation that all things will work all right. You operate a law that can and will put matters right. There is a power within, greater by far than any difficulty that you can ever meet; that power will never fail to see you through.

You may ask, "Can I desire things not ready for me to have?" Can I ask too much of the Law? Does the Law (294) withhold things from me which are not for my good? True desire represents the urge of life, seeking a fuller expression, and is kept alive by continuous expectation of its fulfillment. It brings to us ways and means for its manifestations. The principle explains, "No desire is felt until the supply is ready to appear." No mind can (295) be conscious of a need or of a desire unless the possibility of its fulfillment exists. Your prayer, your desire, and your inner urge are like a magnet and the stronger they are, the stronger the power of your magnet and the greater its attraction. You cannot ask too much of the Law, for it is unlimited and the supply is inexhaustible. You can get only what you can conceive, (296) what you can understand. You can get only the equivalent to what you give. The Law does not withhold any more than mathematics withholds its numbers. You may receive some things that appear not good, but yet (297) good may come through them like mistakes in mathematics. Whereas you make many mistakes, the mistakes enable you by their correction, to better know the Law. After you have made one or several corrections, you will never again repeat the same mistake, so in that way the Law has served you well and has supplied you with a greater knowledge.

(298) "The Lord loveth a cheerful giver"; the Law serveth a free and willing giver. Whatever you give, give it with a free and willing spirit. Give it out with no obligations or dictations attached, then it will come back to you unburdened with obligations or restrictions of any form.

(299) He who gives much receives much. To give your best is to receive the best in ratio to the degree of your giving. The reason why so many people receive little is because they give out so little. They are poverty-stricken because they refuse to give. Whatever the nature of your possessions, give and give abundantly. You are to give of your life, interest, energy, thought, ability, love, **(300)** appreciation, and helpfulness. In giving of your life, thought and love, in doing gladly and well whatever you may be called upon to do, you express your best, and the more you give the more you receive. This does not mean that you are to give to the selfish and thoughtless, but to so order your life as to make a full **(301)** and proper use of your energies, faculties, and talents in useful living. If today your abilities are small and your powers insignificant, begin now to make a more thorough use of them and they will grow.

Recall the story of the Master and his servants to whom he gave each a talent, some two, some three and others more, and from whom he expected a harvest according to their respective endowments. There was greater joy in Heaven over him who had but one talent and used it well than over him who had many talents but failed to employ them in useful service. Hence the servant with one talent took the higher place. In other words, the individual who makes full use of what he has shall be blessed with more and more, for "in what measure ye mete, it shall be measured unto thee again." That is the path of increase. That is the secret of the Law of Receiving.

If the business world accepts the giving of service as the basis of success and progress, can we not accept the same truth in our business of living life? This is not a religious plea; this is good logic, or plain common sense, for if the Law works in one department it surely will work in every department wherever we choose to apply it.

Whatever you desire in the way of health, success, happiness, riches, or power, start toward it, start it on its way by this procedure. The Law works. The results are sure because a natural principle is involved; you may proceed without doubt or fear to desire and to expect all the good you can realize, use, and enjoy. When the mind of man becomes unselfish to the point of yielding to the Law, man has been born anew; for his attitude toward the Law, himself, and his fellowmen has changed, and his affairs take on the character of his newness of thought.

(302)

(303)

(304)

(305)

(306)

GIVING

(307)

To get he had tried, yet his store was still meager.
　　To a wise man he cried, in a voice keen and eager;
"Pray tell me how I may successfully live?"
　　And the wise man replied, "To get you must give."

As to giving he said, "What have I to give?"
　　I've scarce enough bread, and of course one
　　　　must live;
But I would partake of Life's bountiful store.
　　Came the wise man's response; "Then you must
　　　　give more."

The lesson he learned: to get was forgotten,
　　Toward mankind he turned with a love
　　　　newbegotten.
As he gave of himself in unselfish living,
　　Then joy crowned his days, for he grew rich in
　　　　giving.

— *Arthur William Beer*

VI

LAW OF INCREASE

*"Let everything that hath breath praise the
(LAW) Lord. Praise ye the Lord."*

Psalm 150

WITHOUT EXCEPTION I BELIEVE everyone has read or
heard the delightful story of Aladdin and his magic
lamp; how a poor boy had stumbled upon the little
genii who led him to find a dusty old lamp. It was a
magic lamp, and when he rubbed it briskly, a little
man appeared out of a cloud before him and asked to
fill his wishes. We, as children, have always dreamed
of fairies and of the beautiful things in life that we
wished we might have, yet many of our dreams
remained as such because we could do nothing about
them. (308)

In Truth we may not believe in fairies but we know
there is a principle equivalent to the magic lamp. No,
it is not something material that we can carry about
and rub at will to find a little genii to do our bidding;
it is an understanding which enables us to use the Law
more clearly, and in using it we stimulate our good
and bring about much for our pleasure and happiness
that seems like magic or miracles. This understanding
is the act of praising God, the Law, for that which we
desire, and invariably the fulfillment of that desire is
speeded up to almost magic proportion. (309)

This method is, of course, not new. It has been
used throughout the Bible from beginning to end. (310)

Law of Increase

Praise has ever been a common method used to employ the attention, favor, and blessing of God, however one believed in it. In early history we learn that the people would bring their sacrifices and place them on the altar to gain the favor of Jehovah. Following this act they would render their praise in song and ceremony, believing that by so doing they would be favored, their prayers would be granted. Read the song of Moses and note its structure. Read of the fall of Jericho and note the process used by the people, who marched about the city walls until they crumbled and fell, and who became conquerors. Read the last Psalm of David, and in doing so remember that it has been used by the Hebrews for ages and has proven most effective throughout the centuries. The singing of songs or the blowing of trumpets does not bring the results you pray for; nor do you suddenly gain favor with God because of it. The effect of your efforts does not influence God in any sense, but it does influence

(311)

you. It enables you to be lifted up and unconsciously touch the Law and gain its blessing. What has been an unconscious act or an accidental method can become a known fact and a regular means of stimulating your good. If one learns the simple method of praise, that alone will stimulate and increase his good. Jesus once

(312) said, "If one has faith as a grain of mustard seed, he can move mountains." If one can realize the power of praise he can do the same. Praise is complementary to faith. Whereas faith is wisdom and understanding, praise is the application of that understanding. Faith is the boiler that holds a substance of power, whereas

praise is the fuel that generates that power into an active force. If you must constantly watch your boiler and care especially for the fuel that charges it, in order to get the most out of it, then the fuel is a very important part of the machinery. In like manner, faith without praise is but a cold boiler, an inert mass of machinery. It may be nice to look at or to talk about, but of no value more than that until it is put in motion and produces. Praise is a stimulant of the mind. It quickens prayer. It magnetizes all the good around you. It transforms that good into usable, visible substance. (313)

A woman was crying bitterly and praying tearfully to God for her release. The Master hearing her, silenced her and asked, "Is your God a God of tears, of grief and anguish and pain?" Ah, no; God is a giver of joy and peace and happiness and love. You want peace and joy, yet you pray to your Father with tears. If you want black, do you ask for white? If you ask for a fish do you expect a serpent? If you ask for bread, do you expect a stone? You can only get what you expect, for the unchanging Law is ever working to supply you. Prayer should not be one of supplication, pleading, begging, entreating, a sad state. It should be one of claiming, declaring, decreeing, praising and a joyful thanksgiving. (314)

Praise is an avenue of prayer through which the Spirit Law expresses itself. Praise is a broad highway, while all other forms are only feeding arteries. (315) Through this inherent Law, when man praises, he opens himself upward to God. He lifts his consciousness to a higher realm and becomes a greater channel

Law of Increase

to receive the good that is ever waiting to come to him. Praise opens a little door in his mind that enables him to draw closer to God and to be attuned to the Divine forces within and about him. Praise is the shortest route to complete any demonstration and the quickest way to enjoy effectual prayer. Praise expands and opens the mind upward, while its opposite, condemnation, contracts and restricts.

The whole creation responds to praise and is glad.
(316) You may have noted how a trainer, after each performance of his charges, would give them a satisfied pat or some morsel of food they especially liked. That man was wise in using the Law in bringing out the best work from his charges and thereby giving the best performance. You have noticed perhaps how children will glow with gladness and joy when they receive commendation and praise. Those who have trouble with their servants or helpers can learn much by using this method and will find a great difference in the quality and quantity of work produced.

You have experienced at some time, I am sure, this
(317) Law in your affairs. Have you ever had someone to condemn or criticize your efforts when you were trying to please? Did you not feel like folding up within yourself? Perhaps you even felt like quitting the job and letting someone else worry about it. Least of all, such an experience suppressed your interest and zeal, and you did not desire to do better. That is how one reacts when the Law is reversed. Whereas when some-
(318) one praises you for your efforts, you feel like expanding and doing better, trying harder to be more perfect.

Your interest becomes greater because of that pleasure, and with your happiness you bring happiness into your work and all around you. It is a well known fact that even plant life is responsive to praise, for I have seen flowers praised to longer life and beauty.

When we are praised or praise ourselves there is a physical response within our bodies. Doctors tell us that the cells of our body respond to the Law. They (319) seem to know and to expand in strength, in capacity, and even in intelligence. Of course, we know that it is the mind working through every cell that causes the expansion.

There is an invisible ether upon which all thoughts act. As water expands into power when it is heated and retards into a solid mass of ice when it is chilled, the Law of Spirit is reflected in the law of physics. Though we may not sense it or fully understand it, our thoughts are moving continually in this invisible (320) ether, and they are either increasing or diminishing in power and intelligence. When we praise the richness and opulence of God, the Law, our thoughts are greatly increased in the mental atmosphere. This increase affects our being in that it reflects in everything our mind and hands may touch. If we are contracting our (321) thoughts through fear, criticism, and complaint, we reflect that contraction and our results are delayed or frozen.

It has been proven that a failing business can be praised into success. Supposed lost friends have returned their affections when the Law of Praise was used. One man told me that while out driving he (322) heard a clicking noise develop in the rear of his car. He talked to his machine and praised it to get him home safely and without delay. He drove some thirty miles and rolled into the driveway safely. When he tried to move the car further he discovered a broken axle. A woman wrote me stating that she was weary looking at an old carpet that had seen better days and had given good service. She tried the praise method and began to speak kindly to the old rug. Within a few days she had word that a brand new carpet was on its way from Colorado, and that same week she received three smaller rugs equally as new. Her husband, upon seeing the contrast with the new floor covering, decided hurriedly that they must have a new suite of furniture. So, all in all, the Law worked, and by praising the old rug she has a newly furnished living room. Whether the changes are in inanimate things or in individuals, it matters not so long as the desired results are obtained. The Law works without discrimination.

But better still, though praise is good for other persons and things, it is our salvation too. Praise changes our observation, our whole outlook of life. In the past we were in the habit of seeing our weaknesses and failings, as well as the shortcomings of others, but now we see differently. We look for the accomplishments, the good, and the beauty that is worthy of our praise. This, in turn, has a dual effect. It enriches our human self and we are able to radiate praise, joy, courage, and happiness to all who are affected by our influence. It affects our inner self in such a way that our memory

(323)

begins to retain all praiseworthy thoughts sent to it. This sets up a new system of thinking and gradually the old thoughts that were destroying become absorbed in the new ones. Thus it becomes habitual to think praises, and our life takes on the likeness of all good that is worth praising. (324)

Praise with the heart is far more vital and effectual than praise with the head or praise from the lips. Praise does not flatter nor influence God as it does some humans who are turned by superficial praise and applause. Praise is not intended for God. It is intended only for man and is an aid to enable man to lift himself upwards to become attuned with the Law or God. It raises his state of consciousness that he may become more receptive to the good about him and lifts him above the lack of it. Praise raises man's vibration, speeds up his activity, stimulates his faith and contacts a higher realm of thought. (325)

We copy from the Israelites a practice that falls annually. Each year we have a Thanksgiving service, and many think it is for us to express our gratitude for the year past. If you think a moment you can readily see that this is a reversal of the Law of Praise. Such a service should not be a Review, it should be a Preview. That is, a true Thanksgiving service should be an expression of our faith, not in the past, but in the present and in the future to come. Many of us have gotten into a rut. We want our pay in advance. We offer praise after our barns are well filled. If all is going well we are willing to pause to give thanks for our good fortune. Anyone can be grateful with the gift already (326)

(327)

in hand. If conditions are bad, our harvest lean, or trouble besets us, we are apt to forget to praise, and we storm at our failures and often blame God for His neglect.

(328) When one can sing praises in the face of adversity, the adversity will soon disappear. That is not a promise; that is a Law. Learn to render praise, to be thankful for the good at hand, and you will have found the magic lamp of Spirit.

(329) This attitude of mind not only brings forth our desires but it also generates our confidence, strengthens our faith, builds up an assurance for the things to come. Thus to be able to praise when things appear the darkest will invariably force the sunshine through. Our degree of faith in the Law and God is measured before we receive, not afterwards. It is that degree of faith that determines what we shall be capable of receiving.

(330) This is what Jesus knew when He said, "What things soever ye desire, when ye pray, Believe that ye receive them and ye shall have them." Praise is this belief in action, and that action is in the present tense. It is in the Now. Samples of His work show us how He approached His problems. In one case He turned to the patient and asked, "Do you believe ?" To another He questioned, "Do you perceive?" In one of His most trying tests, that of going to the tomb where His beloved friend Lazarus lay dead, we see His approach no different. He stood apart from the mourners and His first words of prayer were, "Father, I thank Thee that Thou hast heard me." What could one be thankful for at a time like that? But the Master knew He was grateful for the answer to His prayer that Lazarus would be restored to life again. Directly He called out in a loud voice, "Lazarus, come forth," and the Book reads that Lazarus stirred in his grave clothes and returned to his body again. (331)

At another time ten lepers called to the Master asking to be healed. He directed them to go show themselves to the priests. Later one of the men came back and expressed his gratitude to Jesus for having been cleansed. Jesus turned to him and asked, "Were there not ten cleansed, but where are the nine?" To the one who touched the Law he said, "Arise, go thy way; thy faith hath made thee whole." One out of ten showed his willingness to return with a grateful heart. He received a permanent healing. Many students fail to repeat their demonstrations because they take too much for granted or they become careless with the Law after they have enjoyed some blessing. One of the first requisites of the Law is that we keep ever an attitude of praise and thanksgiving. If we hope to receive of God's outpouring good we must keep ourselves receptive, and praise is one of the simplest means known to accomplish this. Be ever grateful for the very least of things and the very most will come to you. We must keep our thoughts uplifted always, and praise is the means that will do this. If there is any ingratitude lurking in your mind and heart, begin at once to learn the Psalm of David, Praise ye the (Law) Lord. (332) (333) (334)

As we attune our thoughts to the Law of God, that Law serves us in proportion. This the late Russell

99

(335) Conwell, of the Philadelphia Baptist Temple, must have clearly understood when he called his people to attend a special service of Praise in song and prayer. Anyone in his church who wished prayers for his problems was urged to come, and bring his offerings, leave his name, and state his need. One man of meager means came and asked that his daughter's name be given out. She was a patient in a mental hospital and had to be put away for this reason. The week following the Praise service he called to see his daughter in (336) the hospital and was amazed to have her brought down to him and pronounced healed. A woman brought her jewels and placed them on the altar as her offering. She was afflicted with a physical condition and suffered painfully. She was unable to walk without the aid of her crutches.

Then leaving the church after the service, she tripped and fell on the steps. As she was lifted to her feet she realized she had been healed. Another woman, a widow, came with her mite and asked that she might keep her home, as it was mortgaged and the payments long past due. She went home, but shortly after that it seemed that things were surely going against her. A leak broke out in a water pipe and she was forced to call in a plumber to repair it. How she was ever going to pay him only the Lord would know. When the plumber tore up some floor boards to repair the leak, he uncovered a can of money that her husband had hidden away, and the amount was more than enough to pay the mortgage and the plumber.

Law of Increase

These happenings are all true and can be repeated (337) by anyone who will fulfill the Law as this believing minister has done. The Law cannot fail us when we do not fail it. Learn to turn the Law of Praise upon anything you are praying for and you will see action. Praise is faith in action. A faithful law faithfully observed will ever reward generously the observer. The Law of Praise will lift you from sickness to health; it will raise you from ignorance to intelligence, from poverty to affluence, from weakness to strength, from fear to courage. In fact the Law of Praise will promote you in all things and in all ways. Begin using the Law now.

You haven't much to begin with, you say? Well, (338) neither did Jesus when he had some five thousand hungry souls to feed. He had only five loaves and a few fishes, yet he did something with them. He started action by praising the little at hand and then passed it about. You know the story, and the Master said that what he did we could do, there are no exceptions with the Law. How can it be done? When you learn to take what you have and build upon it, not with scorn and condemnation, but with praise and gratitude, you are (339) working the Law and the Law will give the increase. Praise God that good is everywhere.

VII

LAW OF COMPENSATION

"Whatsoever a man soweth, that shall he also reap."

Gal. 6:7

"THE WORLD OWES ME A LIVING," you hear people say, often with a reckless attitude of determination that they will collect that living in the easiest way they know how. It is current talk at the fireside, across the table, over the radio, and even a political issue that so-and-so should receive a pension in order that he might live on a sum of $200.00 per month, or more or less. Therefore, the statement is familiar to most of us when we hear it. "I don't deserve this," or "How unjustly life has dealt with me," are common expressions of defeat and failure. Why should that person have more than I? I am just as good as he is. We hear these remarks again and again. (340)

The early religious teachings were that justice might be expected in another life. The rich and the powerful, assumed to be the wicked and the overbearing, were bound to receive their punishment in the end. While the poor unfortunate ones, the wretched ones, were to be devoted to their religion and their church; then they were sure to be bountifully rewarded in the next life. The promise of heaven and all that glitters has ever been held over them as a hope of future attainment to make up for their shortcomings on this plane of life, but no such attitude is ever accepted from the viewpoint of Truth when you know the Law. (341) (342)

103

Law of Compensation

(343) Sooner or later we must come face to face with this Law of Compensation, and inevitably our own comes to us, and only what is our own. As we apply it to life and watch its certain results, do we find a balance for the effort of living? Are we satisfied with the good we are receiving? Are we getting fair returns for our efforts? Do we feel that our own has really come to us? Most people are dissatisfied. There are some who even go so far as to say that life is not worth living. The (344) great majority declare that injustice is riotous in the world and more especially in our own lives, that unhappiness, sickness and poverty exist through our living.

(345) In the study of the laws of Truth we learn to apply them so that they will dissolve all our adverse thoughts and conditions. The mistakes of a school boy do not come through the wise operation of the Law; they come through miscalculation. These mistakes will continue so long as he continues using the Law without correction. These mistakes will continue until he changes his way of using the Law. He cannot change the Law to suit his mistakes, but he must change his use of the Law to its correct application. (346) The laws of successful living are the same as the laws of science; the supply and the possibility is ever the same and at hand, but it is our problem to change the use or application of the Law in order to bring about conditions better than those we have had.

(347) The purpose of this lesson is to show you that you can use the Law to lift yourself out of the place where you are to the place where you rightfully belong. Your right place is where you can enjoy success and plenty;

this is natural, as the Law intended; your failure to (348) realize these things is a miscalculation, a mistake. The Law does not need to change. Success or prosperity does not need to be made, it always is. But you, in turn, must change; then your affairs will follow the (349) change. Where do you change? Well, the seat of all movement, the controller of all activity is your thought. "The key to every man is his thought," says Emerson. Why do prisoners strive to get the warden's keys? That they may gain their freedom in the outer (350) world, because there is no other way out. Neither can you be free of your bonds except through the key, through the right use of your thought. The key to successful living is the right adjustment of your thoughts. If your thoughts are constructive and proper, you cannot remain imprisoned. If you are dissatisfied and (351) unhappy, you will be inspired for something better.

If you want prosperity and success but do not strive to change in any way, how can you expect things to be any different? A drunkard never becomes reformed until he decides to stop drinking. If some (352) habit possesses or obsesses you, you are not the master of your life until you decide to change the habit. If you have been brought into the world amidst lack and limitation, you can never get above it until you change your ideas about it. There are many, many people who live and die and never know anything different from what has been handed down to them. Once you have (353) changed your vision, you will change conditions. Only when we cease to recognize a condition do we cease to attract it. The only way we can cease to recognize things is to change our minds about them.

(354) Have you visited several homes and found them all different in some respect? They were neat, tidy, clean, orderly, bright, cheery, or dull, gloomy, disorderly, dusty, uninviting. The home is a reflection of the ruling mind. Its appearance speaks its keeper's mind. If you are working for success, look at the home; if order is the first law, then it must also be your first application. No, lack of money is no excuse for a disorderly home; it can be neat and clean even if you are using store boxes for furniture. If you wish a better home, a finer environment, nicer furnishings, you must alter your mind right where you are to receive better things. It is the little things that count, and many little things make a big thing. It is useless to pray for a new home if you cannot take care of your present one.

(355) A couple operated a fish store in our neighborhood. They neglected to keep the store tidy, were not always courteous in their dealings nor prompt with deliveries. Becoming discouraged from repeated losses they closed out, selling what equity remained. The couple who bought the failing business and the fix-

(356) tures moved in, rolled up their sleeves, scrubbed the room clean and dressed it up with tile boards, making it appear attractive and prosperous. They attracted business at once, established a name for quality food, cleanliness, and courtesy. Their business, in spite of former conditions, steadily grew until it was necessary to lease an adjacent room and increase the size of the store. Some years have passed and these two people have enjoyed an enviable success in the same business

and location where others had failed. The Law helps (357)
those who help themselves. The law of Compensation
always works that way.

When you perform your tasks to the very best of
your ability, or when you are thorough in your work
and do it well, you infallibly bring out the best there is
in you. Otherwise expressed, you grow more capable (358)
and efficient. You become better, and thereby show
your growing superiority. And the Law is that he who
becomes better will attract the better and be given the
greater things to do.

The principle involved is that when you become
too large for your present place you will begin to draw (359)
yourself to something larger; you cannot attract the
better until you first become larger. You must earn
what you receive or you cannot keep it. If an individual appears to do so, it will not continue; for, in accordance with the Law of Compensation, that person will (360)
find his true place. Or, as popularly expressed, "Like
water, he will find his true level," or "You can't keep a
good man down." In truth, the only bar to your
advancement is your own unfitness. In other words,
he who more than fills his present place will, sooner or
later, be advanced. Were it not for this principle, there (361)
could be no progress, no growth, no development, no
evolution.

If the office is all cluttered up with papers, maga-
zines, and bundles, if the boss's desk is stacked with
mail, and some a week old, the office force is careless.
The business reflects the mind of the organization. The (362)
organization reflects the mind of its chief. Where do

we go to find the cause of any leaks? We go to the head; we change his ideas, and the whole organization is converted directly. Change the mind of the general and you have changed the route and purpose of the whole army.

(363) To blame your difficulty on outer conditions or on other people is not correct. It is not the Law, it is You who are wrong. You have a snag in your mentality somewhere. Check back and readjust your ideas; they are creating and bringing forth your conditions. "Do (364) men gather grapes of thorns, or figs of thistles?" Jesus included this Law as a supreme factor in His doctrine. "Give and it shall be given unto you. Judge not that ye be not judged. With what measure ye mete, it shall be measured unto you." And Paul said, "Whatsoever a man soweth, that shall he also reap."

(365) The Law that we reap what we sow is mathematically accurate. Each experience through which we pass operates ultimately for our good. If we attract the unpleasant, it is often because some dormant or neglected phase of our nature needs to be awakened and developed; also, we learn from the experience to cre- (366) ate something better. Hence the degree of contentment and satisfaction attained in whatever sphere of life we may dwell is largely dependent upon our ability to use constructively the experiences of life; for, in every case, the Law of Attraction will only bring what may (367) serve us in our upward development. To interpret this Law in a simple form, it should be stated that whatever we attract we require, and whatever we need is always good. This is a correct attitude to adopt,

Law of Compensation

because all experience is for our good and we must be able to see it in that light.

While pursuing this practice you may not always (368) secure the precise form of results desired, but you will steadily build up your mind and character in harmony, beauty, and strength; because all such effort to realize the ideal is highly constructive and develops in you the very qualities and conditions repeatedly pictured in mind. Clear, strong, positive thought along ideal lines is a wonderful preventive of morbid mental (369) states and negative thinking, which leads to misdirected actions and conditions of weakness, misfortune, discord, and trouble. By constantly trying to meet and to deal with everything on its better side and to use the good it may contain to promote improvements, you (370) are giving the whole attention to the Ideal and cooperating with the Law's fundamental purpose.

Crowd out all inferior thoughts by superior thoughts, evil thoughts by good thoughts, ugly (371) thoughts by beautiful thoughts, distressing thoughts by pleasant thoughts, and you will begin to overcome the growth of all negative and confused states of wrong and discord. In other words, learn to think constructively of all persons, all things, all events, and all circumstances. Appraise them from the ideal point of (372) view. As you do this you will gradually transform your whole existence for the better. These are the means whereby you may steadily promote your welfare and advancement. As you train yourself to mentally look for the good, you will move towards the (373) good; and, as you form higher and larger conceptions

Law of Compensation

of the good, these elements will begin to find expression in your words, acts, character, person, talents, powers, attainments, and achievements; that is, all things in your life will commence to improve as the direct result of your improved thinking. This process

(374)   does not imply, however, that you are to ignore the wrongs of life, the empty places, and the undeveloped states of being; but that you are to think right through and beyond them toward the hidden Good or the Principle within that is ever seeking a higher and fuller expression. You will, therefore, cease to condemn and to criticize in a destructive manner; instead,

(375)   you will seek to bring out the good in yourself and in others, and to discover and develop the greater possibilities everywhere.

Whatever we possess today is our just reward. Very often it does not make us happy; we are dissatis-

(376)   fied with it, but still it remains ours. This fact would prove hopelessly discouraging were it not for a great truth that teaches us how to be free from every difficulty, released from all bonds, absolved from every debt. If you want success in living life, you must exercise an intelligent discrimination of your thoughts. When you talk hard times, money scarcity, limitation,

(377)   you are sowing that type of seed. What kind of harvest do you expect to get? If the farmer sowed thistle seed, and then complained that his field did not bring forth wheat, you would say, "Foolish man! Didn't he know he could only expect what he had planted?" Never make an assertion, no matter how real it seems to be to you, if you do not want it reproduced or continued in

your life. Do not say money is scarce; the very statement will send money away from you. Do not say (378) times are hard; this will tighten your purse strings so tight that even God will not be able to slip in another coin. Do not say you are not loved, or not interested in other people's lives. Truly you will lose their interest and their love.

The Spiritual Supply from which the visible comes is never depleted. It never runs out. It is with you all (379) the time. It will yield according to your demand upon it. It is not affected by your ignorant or blind talk of lack or loss; only you are the one affected, and you control your demonstration with your thought. The unfailing Resource is willing to give, it has no choice (380) in the matter; if you continue to pour out your thoughts into this substance, this will prosper you. Turn the energy of your mind upon ideas of plenty, love, happiness, joy, health, and they, in turn, will appear.

If you want a better home, make the one you have as nice as you can. If you want new furnishings, new clothing, don't condemn or belittle what you have, but (381) enjoy them to the fullest. If you want a position or a new one, get yourself in readiness to fill that position or improve the one where you are. Hence, your failure to meet your demands of life is not a failure of the material; it is but a failure within yourself of the lack of understanding or the lack of application. No matter (382) what your problem is, the Law can work it out, but you must adjust your thinking to work with the Law. Do not expect that in just a few moments or a few applications you will realize a full consciousness of

111

plenty. A builder does not erect a beautiful spire or
(383) dome to a million dollar cathedral without founda-
tion; he must first have support to hold that spire aloft.
He builds walls and cross braces to hold each wall,
and each wall is built slowly and perfectly, stone by
stone. You must realize that by working and proving
the Law, you do so step by step, with each step bringing you closer to your goal.

In Philadelphia a man boasted that he was a suc-
(384) cess; he rose above his competitors; he drove them off
the street, some of them out of business. He founded
his business upon competition, but I learned only
recently that his business had dwindled down to the
place where he was forced to close out and move to a
smaller town. The Law of Compensation works slow-
(385) ly but surely; one cannot build upon the substance or
the virtue that another has created. You can only build
on that which you create. Competition in business is a
rivalry, or strife, for two or more people. Fearing there
is not enough for all, they fight with one another to get
all they can. Don't fear your neighbor is getting more
out of life than you are; don't try to compete with anyone or anything. It has been said that competition is
the spirit of business, but I do not think that competition in the form of rivalry and strife, of arguing and
fighting and lying about each other and each other's
business, is the right spirit. I know it is not. Rather
than call competition the spirit of business, let us call
it compensation. Compensation means equal returns
(386) for that which is given; it means a balance of that quality or service that is extended to another. I am certain

that if you conduct your life, which is your business, along the path of compensation rather than competition, you will find it more enjoyable to compare your quality and service with another. The better your service, the greater the reward, the more business you will attract. If you follow this Law, you will find that it is the golden rule in any life or in any business. You will (387) be certain to succeed no matter if there are other so-called competitors seeking business in the same block. If you are not succeeding, if you lack any good thing, look more closely to the cause. It is not outside; it is (388) somewhere within. See where you fail to use the Law correctly or where you fail in your consciousness to think rightly. There are three points common in every-day life where one may fall into a snare and a delusion.

First of all: DO YOU EXPECT SOMETHING FOR NOTHING? Does it make you feel good, pleased, when you get (389) something without paying for it? If so, you are violating the Law. Your returns will always be unsatisfactory. No matter where you go, be willing to pay your way. Have you known some people who hang back when you go out for an evening's entertainment? They stand back and let the other fellow pay for the show. People like that lose hundreds of dollars when they try to save themselves a paltry fifty cents. The quality of thought they entertain repels many dollars they rightly could attract. If you, knowingly, cheat another one of a dollar, it may cost you many dollars for the mistake.

Second: Do you hunt for things that are called cheap? ARE YOU A BARGAIN HUNTER? Cheap thoughts can only bring cheap returns. You who wait for bar-

Law of Compensation

(390) gain days will always have to take bargains, but remember, there are no bargains in life. If you have gained monetarily, you may have lost in other ways. You place yourself in a vibration that lowers your present state. It forces you below your proper level. It limits your thought to a state where you support underselling, cutting, bankruptcy and dishonesty on (391) the part of the seller. He must lie, or deceive, or cheat somehow about the price of the bargain or some other article, because he is in business to make a fair profit. Thus, you become a party to the violation and come under its penalty.

Third: DO YOU BEGRUDGE SPENDING MONEY? Do You Hate To Pay Your Bills? Release your money cheerful- (392) ly even if it be the last dollar you have. Decide what your need is; if it is of more value than the dollar in your purse, then spend the dollar cheerfully. In this way you comply with a law. Often when we get to a low level we begin to tighten up on our purse strings. We begin to hold back. This is like closing the faucet, limiting the supply from pouring in to you. I remem- ber a man telling of a time when he had an urgent need for a thousand dollars. He had but a ten dollar bill in his purse and he was holding on to that bill like (393) a drowning man to a straw. For days, he said, he car- ried it about with him, afraid to spend it for fear of being broke. Suddenly it occurred to him that he was pinning his faith more on the ten dollars than he was on the true source of supply. He was closing his faucet with a mere ten dollar bill; it had grown to become a fearful obstruction. When he realized this truth, he sat

Law of Compensation

down at once and mailed the bill to a nearby church, and following the release of the bill, supply began to flow in to him. Before that week was out, he received his thousand dollars, enough to pay the month's obligations. He added, "Never since has supply failed to flow to me, for I learned my lesson."

The Law inevitably produces its own exactness as a rule of action. It is a Divine Law and tolerates no violation. It does not bring forth figs from thistles. If man (394) misuses the Laws of harmony, health, or supply, the Law of Compensation becomes manifest.

We are free agents to choose the method of procedure in our life. The Law is infinite, and through its expressions all things are possible to us. Every time we (395) choose a good thought, we make a good investment.

What is life giving you today? Health, happiness, and abundance; or sickness, misery, and lack? Whatever it is, it is your own. It belongs to no one else but you. You make your investments and you are (396) daily enjoying the profits or losses. If you are dissatisfied with your investment, it may be wise for you to note what you invested. Only your own can come to you, and be sure that all that is yours will become manifest. It is your responsibility; no other person may share it. Your own and all of your own will come to you.

> "I rave no more 'gainst time or fate,
> For, lo, my own shall come to me."
>
> *--John Burroughs*

115

VIII

LAW OF NON-RESISTANCE

"But I say unto you; That ye resist not evil."
Matt. 5:39

OUR INTEREST IN THIS LAW of Truth is especially oppor-
tune at this time when, to many earnest students, there
seems to be so much in the world to be met, which
apparently cannot be met unless some resistance is set
up. Sin and sickness seem to have multiplied despite
all the efforts made to counteract them. Resistance as a
means of securing peace and harmony is a mistaken
and misleading idea. True harmony cannot come from
inharmony, nor peace from discord. Resistance fails
because it is not in accord with harmony and order,
which is the Law.

(397)

The Master's doctrine, that ye resist not evil, seems
a paradox to some of us. It seems contrary to the natural reactions of a body, for when we meet with opposition it seems natural to steel our energies, collect our
wits, and use whatever means we have to outwit and
break down the opposition. Yet, as contrary as it may
seem in one sense, when it pertains to the more serious
things in life, we are unconsciously using the Law in
the trivial and material things. There are so many
other names given to this Law that we may not recognize it always as the primal Law of Non-Resistance.

(398)

Law of Non-Resistance

(399) For example, in our business world we hear about the psychology of salesmanship, service, credit, free deliveries, expert advisers and every other aid conceivable that will help us find the right pots and pans for the kitchen, the proper style and color of a crib for the nursery, the chair for the fireplace, and the accessories that are so necessary to show off the living room effectively. In fact, there is one business house that advertises, WE HAVE EVERYTHING UNDER THE SUN, so no matter what you need you can find it there. This is good business, you say, and the department heads know business is good as long as they use this law.

(400) Why do you suppose they keep the doors wide open in the stores where you shop? Certainly it is not to let fresh air in. It is to let prosperity come in to them without even having to swing open the doors. Have you ever noticed the number of people who walk through an open door in comparison to the number who open a door? Have you ever wondered why stores like the "5 and 10" or the "25 cents to dollar" stores prefer to use the basement instead of a second floor? It is easier for people to walk down stairs than to climb up. Of course, they eventually walk up the steps when they come out, but it is the first thought of the people that directs them to go down. You will note that this psychology is used freely in any large business. They often employ men and women to study ways and means to interest and attract customers. They study the Law of Non-Resistance and the simple ways it can be used upon the public.

Law of Non-Resistance

A salesman will study the ways and means of selling an article. He will approach a customer and present his product in a careful manner. He will bring out (401) comparison with other similar products, he will praise his product and show all of its good points, trying all the while to avert any objection or argument in the customer's mind. In this manner he builds up a positive sales talk and leads his customer to a positive acceptance. He will get the customer to say "yes" to so many things that before the customer is aware of his action, he is signing a check or a contract. The whole of salesmanship is built on the Law of Non-Resistance. Successful business houses everywhere are using it. Department stores are the outgrowth of its use. When our grandparents went shopping with their baskets, there were many shops visited before they finished. Today we can use the phone and order our list of supplies, very likely from one store. Mail order houses are dependent upon this method. It is in this way that they make is easy for prosperity to come to them.

Business houses do not employ the only salesmen, for everyone is a salesman of some kind. Whether we realize it or not, we are ever selling ourselves to our friends for approval or disapproval. We are ever striv- (402) ing to put forth our best self, and inwardly want our friends to see us in that light. A young man wishing to meet that certain young lady will try every means to gain an introduction. Then he will put his best foot forward, act his best, make the most pleasing impression. Why all this extra effort, you ask? Because he wants to make it easy for the fair lady to like him and wish to

119

know him better. He is trying to sell her the idea that he is her best choice for a companion and friend. He may be unconsciously using the Law of Non-Resistance as far as he knows.

(403) Why does this young man put forth his best side? Oh, you say, that is only natural, it is a habit or a custom. That is true, yet we become so governed by habit and custom that there are times when we, in working for prosperity and good health, unconsciously put opposition in our path through this force of habit.

(404) There are some who may be working to gain success and to bring forth an increase of supply or material wealth and yet have gotten into the habit of talking and fearing hard times. We may talk about our neighbor or criticize the method he used to get ahead. We may fear business conditions and when we see the graph take a downward swing we fear for our investments and our job. When we do these things we are very foolish. In fact, as foolish as a merchant who

(405) advertised extensively that on a certain day he would inaugurate the biggest sale of the year. After getting his patrons all keyed up for the bargains promised, he barred the doors and closed everyone out. For such an act the patrons thought he must have gone crazy or else he did not want any business to come to him.

(406) Well, call him what you will, but some people are just as crazy at times when they want supply and prosperity to come to them and then bar the way with their conversations of poverty and discord. I don't say they are crazy, but I know they haven't learned how to think right; nor are they wise to the Law when they

choke off their influx of good with negative chatter. **(407)**
One student wrote me and said, "I am working hard
over limitation, for I have had enough of it." My
answer to her was, "Cease working over limitation
and work only for prosperity." The Law does not
require us to work over or against the things we do
not want but it does require us to work with and for **(408)**
that which we do want. We dare not give our time,
thought and energy to that which is opposed to what
we want. That is setting up a resistance contrary to the
Law and barring the way for our good to come in.
How, then, shall we work for prosperity? By being **(409)**
non-resistant and in agreement with all that is prosperous and using every means at our command to
make it easy for prosperity to come in.

Water is very powerful, yet it is a perfect nonresis-
tant element. We can see where it has worn away the **(410)**
hardest rock. We have seen it sweep everything before
its torrential outburst. Bridges, buildings, trees, nothing can withstand its force. Yet, note how the great
river begins. It starts with a small stream or brook high
up in the mountains where the ice and snow feed it in
the springtime. Note also that it is a very crooked little
stream, nothing like the great river it finally flows into.
You see the little stream of water run into a huge boul-
der, a fallen tree, or debris made up of bushes,
decayed leaves, and the like. Does the little stream
stop with the obstacle and wait for its force to build up
so that it can push the opposition from its path? No,
the little stream is not interested so much in the boul-
der or tree as it is in hurrying along and reaching a

Law of Non-Resistance

larger stream, a river, and then the mighty ocean. It does not waste any time with the obstacle, but quietly works its way around the interference and hurries on. It is urged to meet a river and then to be a part of the mighty ocean. Thus, we see that little stream wind its way round and round many crooks and turns, but every turn takes it nearer its goal.

(411) Some people, unwise to Nature's method, set up a different one. When they meet an obstacle they stop their progress to collect their forces and put up a fight to remove it. This resistance they set up causes friction. Friction causes an irritation and an inflammation. For this reason many people's lives are hard and exacting. The waste of human energy is appalling. People in every walk of life are breaking down and wearing out like obsolete machinery. Remember, it is not the movement of a machine that wears it beyond use and (412) service, it is FRICTION. Friction is opposition and resistance.

If we go through life fighting, opposing, resisting, arguing, we are bound to meet with many obstacles and likely become so occupied fighting them that we lose sight of our real objective. If we are always getting steeled for the next opposition or trouble we can expect plenty of it. Whereas if we strive to make little of the obstacle and keep our minds on the objective or (413) the desire we set out to gain, we may have to wind around and around, but if we persevere we will ultimately win. We will reach the goal.

Another lesson we may learn from the stream is (414) that when it is small and struggling it has the most difficult time. In the beginning it will have so many obstacles across its path that it is ever winding around to avoid direct opposition. Silently it uses the Law to be non-resistant and it grows stronger in force and volume. When it becomes a larger stream and then a river its path is more direct and the obstacles become less and less. Then it is not far from the mighty ocean. Students are like that. They have their hardest tests and delays while they are yet weak in power and understanding. As they strike out on a new path in (415) Truth, the obstacles and tests will be plentiful. The wise ones will not fight the obstacles, but bless them and go on. As they go on with faith and assurance, they grow stronger and become like a great stream and river. Their course becomes more direct, their understanding is of greater depth and the mighty ocean, their ultimate objective, is not far from them.

A woman recently asked for help to meet her problem. She explained that her home was mortgaged and (416) it was near time for her to make a payment, but the funds were lacking. She had converted her home into a rooming house, hoping to get money enough to live on, but there was the difficulty. She could not keep her roomers because they were so quarrelsome and critical. The house was always in an uproar, no one was content, and she was ill in mind from the strain and anxiety.

It was explained that she must use the Law. She must not oppose the good, but strive to work with it. (417) With all the friction and confusion in the home, she must go back and use the Law of Non-Resistance. This she tried to do, but whereas she had been so exacting and unkind, she found it rather hard to be non-resistant. That evening as she entered the dining room, she greeted her people with a smile. The folks were so startled at the sudden change that they could hardly eat for wondering. That smile was the first smile some had ever seen from her, and others declared it was the first time in months that they remembered. One man was heard to utter when she had gone to the kitchen to fix the dessert, "The old lady is going soft." And more thought so later that evening when they heard her greet one young man who had gotten back in his rent and who was trying to slip up to his room without being seen. She greeted him pleasantly and said she was sorry he had missed his dinner.

After a few weeks of this new plan the woman began to enjoy it. She had become changed within herself. She saw her folks in a different light. Instead of thinking them to be cheats, liars, and a quarrelsome lot, she saw good in them and she grew to like them more and more as one big family. They, too, became different. The family gathering at the table was looked forward to as a happy time and had grown to its capacity. Others had asked to have a room if and when a vacancy occurred. Even the young man who had tried to dodge her because of his arrearage had entered into the spirit of the new home and was able to get a job and paid up in full. Needless to say, the payments on the mortgage were met and the home was saved for the widow. She did as she was instructed. She became non-resistant to the good. She made light of the many obstacles and confusion that

(418)

124

appeared, and slowly worked around them. She held in mind her objective. This in turn melted down the hardness within herself and then reached others. Though she appeared to be going soft to some, in doing so she reached her goal and was victorious.

In another verse Jesus expressed the Law more simply; He said: "I say unto you, love your enemies; (419) bless them that curse you; do good to them that hate you; pray for them that despitefully use you." In studying this statement one might at first think the Master was favoring the enemies, the opponents. Not (420) at all; Jesus was speaking to all who desire to use the Law. To extend a loving thought to anyone or anything removes the opposition and enmity that once seemed there. This removal must first be in the person's consciousness. Once the thought of enmity is removed from your consciousness you will not attract (421) the same condition again. Do good to them that hate you because in doing good you are raised above the thought of hate and hate then cannot touch your life. Bless them that curse you and pray for them that misuse you. Why? Blessing calls forth the highest good within you. The highest good within you can only attract the highest good from another. To attract such good you are running around all opposition and abuse. Thus to live the Law with others about you (422) does not especially favor the others so much as it favors you. It affects others in that it takes away from them their weapons of hate, malice, revenge and the like, and their love and interest will be reciprocal with yours.

Law of Non-Resistance

(423) If a man resists a situation, he will have it always with him. If he tries to run away from it, like a shadow it follows him, and repeatedly he will meet it again. If he ignores the hardness of the condition and fearlessly works around it, he will find a time when that hard condition will have been absorbed and removed. Accept the condition as some evidence of good. Look for that good, and by being acceptable to it more and more evidence of it appears.

(424) "Agree with thy adversary" is another way of saying that nothing worthwhile and lasting is ever gained by argument. He who is convinced against his will is of the same opinion still. To disagree with one only causes that one to put on his full armor, to collect all his forces in opposition to yours. To agree with your worthy opponent leaves him defenseless and without need of his armament. To offer no resistance makes it easy for one to be amicable, and he who thought himself your enemy will find it a pleasure and a privilege to be a friend.

(425) "Blessed are the meek" may seem literally to support those kindly timid souls who are an easy prey for their more aggressive brothers. Rather, it refers to the one who is able to follow the Law of Non-Resistance to the point of inheriting the earth and all things thereof. To be meek does not mean to be an easy mark nor to be a door mat for anyone to walk over. I have heard it said that in this day one cannot be a real Christian and be easy and forgiving. In this day one must be on **(426)** guard to protect one's rights from being overridden by the stronger and more abusive. One does not know what is fully required of a true Christian if he thinks this. We are not asked to be a martyr for our belief; nor is it unchristian to be able to speak out fearlessly and positively.

We need not be an easy mark nor a door mat for anyone, for there is a greater power to be reckoned with, the power of the Law when you use it. Yet this does not make us like a pugilist, but a master. This does not require us to be hardboiled and boisterous in order that we may attain our rights. Our rights when they are righteous will uphold themselves, they are their own defense. They do not need us nor anyone to fight their battles. Now the Law reads that "WE ATTRACT WHAT WE EXPECT," so if one believes he is an easy mark, a door mat, a weakling, if he expects to suffer imposition and must resort to warlike means for his protection, then "they that take the sword shall perish by the sword." The Law of life reacts upon man according to his understanding and application. (427) (428)

To be meek does not mean that we are submissive to the conditions of discord and disorder. We are meek only to the Law. Such meekness gives us the power of Spirit. Jesus was so strong in Spirit that His spoken word was like a two-edged sword, it beat welts upon the intruder like a whip lash. Jesus, though a humble man, was no example of weakness. When He spoke as one with authority to the Scribes or cleared the Temple of the money changers, He showed a strength that was a delight to His disciples to the extent that they implored Him to be their king. Do not confuse meekness with weakness. Nature eliminates (429) (430)

127

Law of Non-Resistance

(431) weakness, and so she should. Weakness ever creates weakness. This brings on deterioration and finally death and decay. To live wisely one must be strong and positive, though righteously meek. Such strength is not measured in physical brawn and muscle, but in mind and spirit. NO ONE CAN BE TRULY MEEK WHO IS NOT STRONG AND SPIRITED.

(432) Meekness, then, is that strength appropriated when you do not argue, when you do not become angry or boastful and proud, when you do not insist upon having your rights in a quarrelsome manner. Meekness is the steel of one's nature. It is enduring. Meekness is the strength by which you win an argument by refusing to argue. When differences of opinion arise and your opinion is right, the real victory lies in the fact that right is right, regardless of what others may say about it.

(433) In science we recognize the spirit of meekness as cooperativeness, persistent application, accurate computation, perfect harmony, symmetry of design and color, and so forth. Possibly the simplest illustration can be seen in our application of the law in Nature. We exercise the spirit of meekness in accepting the terms of nature, and the more fully we cooperate or submit to her, the more abundantly we are blessed. We carefully select the best seed and plant it in the right place at the proper time and in the most fertile soil. Careful are we to water and cultivate the growing plant to

(434) insure a bountiful yield. Why are we so careful, so particular, so non-resistant to obey nature's law? Is it because we are weaklings, crave excessive work, and

128

in general, simpletons because of the utmost care and attention we are obliged to give? Only he who does not meet the law with non-resistance is foolish. With whatever degree the wise one meets the law with meekness, nonresistance, so will he be benefited. (435) Thus, as man applies the spirit of meekness to the principles of his daily life, not to the conditions, so will he be proportionately blessed.

When perplexed, remember the little stream of water and how determined it is to reach the mighty ocean. Be that determined to reach and realize all the (436) good that is awaiting you. Why delay its benefits by putting obstacles into your stream of prosperity? Let us come over the path of non-resistance. Every worried thought, every fear, doubt, complaint, argument, and angry thought are but so many boulders, large and small, that you cast into your stream. These tend to change your course and to lengthen the time for your goal to be reached. Unite your forces for good with the good that is seeking you. Remove and dissolve every obstacle by blessing it and being willing to understand it. Mark it no longer a stumbling block, but a stepping stone, leading to your highest good.

IX

LAW OF FORGIVENESS

"Forgive, and ye shall be forgiven."
Luke 6:37

THERE ARE CRUCIAL THINGS in life that call for great human qualities. Our present fear is that man will not be big enough to meet the demands of the day. A lack of large character equipment is a real peril at all times. It is here and now that the world needs the help of a Master such as Jesus the Christ. **(437)**

Jesus taught bigness of character to His followers. With such bigness within Himself He was more than a Preacher. He was a Teacher Supreme. He not only pointed the way, but He went forward and showed the way. In the hours of great stress He showed Himself mightier than Pilate, the Governor of all Judea, or Caiaphas, the High Priest and head of the Church, or any and all of the accusing Scribes and Pharisees. It is true that for a moment they had power over His body and tried Him and condemned Him to be crucified, the maximum sentence that could be given anyone, but through it all His mind and Spirit commanded them. They dragged Him through the streets bound as a prisoner, they nailed Him to a cross on the hill of Calvary, but He, looking down upon them and seeing their smallness of mind, cried out, "Father, forgive them; for they know not what they do." A man who is great enough to forgive is always greater than the forgiven. He is superior. He is greater than his adversary. **(439)**

(438)

131

Law of Forgiveness

(440) Peter, the disciple, was greatly perplexed one time while listening to one of the many lessons of the Master. He raised the question which is the basis of this lesson. Turning to Jesus he asked: "Lord, how often shall my brother sin against me, and I forgive him, until seven times?" Now this was a generous gesture on his part, for the Jewish law which he had known allowed a man to be forgiven three times. This was more than twice the grace that the law allowed, so Peter must have felt the Lord would be pleased with his extension of forgiveness. But he found himself more perplexed when Jesus answered, "I say not unto thee until seven times, but until seventy times seven." Such a period would be indefinitely, so by that answer there are no limits or restrictions to the Spirit graces. The quality of forgiveness must be as limitless as Faith, Hope and Love.

(441) The Teachings of Jesus in reference to man's power to forgive sins are, I believe, among the least understood of all the Commands. As a rule there is a separation made between sin and its many effects. When a man sins we have been taught to think that this was a job for the minister, and so he is called to pray for the sinner. When a man becomes sick and distressed in mind and body from the effects of the sins he committed, we call for a doctor. The doctor in turn endeavors to treat or repair the body and arrest the suffering. This, at best, we know is but a temporary measure, for (442) no real healing or permanent cure can be effected until the doctor and the minister work together.

Law of Forgiveness

Jesus was the Master Physician in that He dealt with sin and sickness jointly. When they brought a man to Him who had been sick with palsy, Jesus spoke of forgiving the man's sins in order to heal him. **(443)** The people who had gathered around and heard Him speak, questioned His actions. They said, "Who is this that speaketh blasphemies? Who can forgive sins but God alone?" They did not understand how He could consider sin as a cause of palsy. But there are some no further advanced today who still want to believe that **(444)** such a disease is caused by a physical or an organic disorder, rather than to accept the possibility of it being a mental or spiritual laxity.

Jesus plainly taught that if ye forgive sin the effect of such an act of forgiveness would become absorbed **(445)** with natural and healthy ideas much the same as the blackest of night is absorbed with the dawn of light. The blackness disappears and the light of day shines upon all alike. When healthy and natural ideas fill the mind the body takes on a like condition. Thus our progressive men and women who are turning to a broad- **(446)** er field of study and are effecting healings through mental and spiritual processes are not giving us anything new. They are merely catching up with the facts of the Master and are practicing His methods and teachings more liberally.

Jesus taught that the originating place of every act was in the mind. He said, in brief, that where there is **(447)** lust in the heart, there is a sin; though the act may never be committed. At another place He speaks of the

133

origin of sin being in the mind first before the act is committed. "For from within," He said, "out of the heart of man, proceed evil thoughts, adulteries, murders, thefts, deceit, blasphemy, pride, foolishness. All these evil things come from within, and they defile the man."

(448) Scientists accept the Truth that the body of man is moved by the mind, that all its functioning is governed by a ruling thought, whether that thought is subjective or objective, whether it is conscious or unconscious. Those who study the mental processes find that all the conditions of the body are created or caused by the mind. It is known that creation in any

(449) and every form is governed by and subject to a law. Hence, when one misuses, inverts, or violates a law, this mistake is called a Sin. A sin is a mistake, a misunderstanding, and a misjudgment. A mistake is falling short of, or disobeying the law, whether that law be mechanical or spiritual. Correction is the only method

(450) of adjustment or of appeasing the law. Thus, repentance and forgiveness are the only means available to alter and correct the mistake. They are the only means of liberating man from suffering the painful consequences of a mistake. They are the only means that will enable him to become in accord or in harmony with the law. Forgiveness of sin means that we must forgive, forsake, and forget that thought or person or condition which prompted the sin. It means to abandon or let go of the thing you ought not do. To abandon or release the wrong thoughts or idea is to be absolved and liberated from its sinful effects.

Law of Forgiveness

Forgiveness is the first requirement which permits man to be in harmony with the Law of his being.

"Who can tell what that Law is?" we may ask. Anyone who studies man as both a mental and a physical being can know the Law. If he were to try to learn the Law by studying the physical actions or the results of the Sin alone, it would lead to nowhere. He would be running around in circles, and that would be useless and futile. If he will go deeper and study the causes and that which prompted the sin, he will get results. He must analyze the case and search for some harbored, hidden, and forgotten shock or condition that would have caused the illness. Then, unless this harbored thought is uprooted from the unconscious mind or memory, this condition will continue to appear again and again in spite of all the surface remedies that may be applied to arrest the pain. Like weeds in your garden, if you go about and cut them off each time they appear before your eyes, they may be cut off for a time, but, because they were not pulled out root and all, they will sprout again. Weeds must be pulled out completely to be destroyed and permanently removed.

A noted physician, talking before a group of other medical men on this very subject of thought being the source of disease, was recorded as having said in his concluding remarks, "Abnormal tumors and cancers are due to a long period of suppressed grief and anxiety." Another way of saying this is that such diseases are due to a lot of sinful thoughts getting bottled up and suppressed within our minds. If this state is so

(451)

(452)

(453)

(454)

(455)

destroying, it might be wise for us to probe into our own selves and note the effect our emotions have upon the physical organism. Then let us seek by every means at our command to overcome, abandon, and forsake every emotional tug that has a debilitating and disturbing effect.

(456) Another leading psychiatrist has said, "Most of the cases of mental disorder of a functional type are due to a sense of guilt." There are some harbored and congested thoughts that need forgiveness. Usually a sick mind fears to release them or to forgive them. This is natural, for if they were able to release and forgive the fearful thoughts they would no longer be sick minded.

(457) Professor Gates of the Psychological Laboratory of Washington, D.C., in an experiment testing the emotions and the reactions of the body, found some interesting results. He found some forty bad emotions, and many more that were good. Of all the bad emotions he said the reaction of guilt was the worst. This deduction was gained by a chemical analysis of the perspiration taken from the body. A small quantity of perspiration was taken from each emotional reaction and tested. The bad emotion showed a strong acid test. Now if you put some acid on your flesh you know what will happen. The acid will burn, and if allowed to continue to burn it will prove painful and destroy the very tissue of your flesh. It is just such a chemical (458) reaction that is affecting the tissue and organism of the body when these destroying thoughts are allowed to harbor within and generate a poison which weakens and eventually destroys the body.

A wise physician one day had a caller who, as he put it, had gone the round of the doctors and sanitari- (459) ums, but with it all was as yet not healed. In fact, he was growing worse, and in addition to the original malady, he had an increasing condition of melancholia and with suicidal tendency. The physician, knowing that he had gone the rounds and had had medical care, decided to approach the case from a mental angle. He questioned and studied each answer with care. After a time he gained the confidence of his patient and learned the real secret cause of his long illness.

Many years before, this man and his brother were business partners, and the man had appropriated and lost some money that rightfully belonged to his brother. It was used in such a way that his brother could not have found this out even if he had investigated. They later severed business connections and he retired from that work, but, as he put it, he could never forgive himself for taking the money. He wanted to return it, but could not do so without the brother learning the truth. He said it was not the fear of legal punishment that tormented him so much, but the possible loss of his brother's affection. They had always been inseparable and devoted. It was for this reason that he feared to confess his guilt and make amends in whatever way he could.

The physician explained that the thing to do was to relieve this hidden pressure. The only way to do it was to call on his brother and make a clean breast of (460) the whole affair. The patient, not equal to the suggestion, went home to think it over. Three days later he called the physician, stating that he had spent three dreadful days and sleepless nights battling with himself, and had decided to visit his brother. He was in such a mental state that he knew his brother's treatment, once he learned he was a thief, could be no worse than the misery he was suffering. He told his brother the story, and to his surprise, the brother threw his arms about him and rejoiced with him that it was cleared from his mind. It was a joyful time for **(461)** them, for that cloud, the only cloud in their lives, had disappeared. The skies were clear again and the restoration of the health of the patient was miraculous to those who did not understand what had been cleared away.

Through repentance and forgiveness the man was able to do as Jesus had commanded the woman He was called upon to judge, "Go thy way and sin no more." The rooted sorrow had been plucked from his memory. His mind was free to think on healthy, **(462)** happy and joyful thoughts. This allowed his body to be quickly healed. To some it may have seemed like a miracle, but not at all; it was a natural law operating in a natural, unrestricted way.

Facing such indisputable facts we can understand more fully why Jesus so often spoke of forgiving sin. **(463)** He knew the law of forgiveness and He knew how vitally important a part it played in every man's life. The more we study it, the more amazed we become at its simplicity and accuracy of fulfillment. We are to forsake, for as Solomon tells us, "A SIN FORSAKEN IS A

SIN FORGIVEN, " to forgive, to release some part of our disposition that is not an asset nor a pleasure to others around us. In turn, we are repairing the breach where we have missed the mark, made a mistake, or sinned. Weeds do not remove themselves in time. Instead they will increase and grow stronger until they choke out the flower. The same thing is true of our sinful thoughts. In the garden of our memory they must be plucked out, cast out, and destroyed so that only flowers of healthy and happy thoughts may grow. **(464)**

A man may have the habit of excessive drinking, and is not only miserable within himself, but causes much unhappiness in his home. He desires to overcome the sinful habit. He is given every aid from his friends and loved ones to help him resist the desire and the craving for drink. Time after time he rises above the temptation, and then he fails. Repeatedly his family forgives him and encourages him to battle on. Finally he reaches the place when he no longer has the craving, then he is able to forsake the desire for drink and overcome its sinful effects. Then he has forsaken, not the drink alone, but the desire for the drink. When man forsakes the idea that prompts the desire and brings about the physical action, then and not until then does the Law forgive and lift him from its debilitating effect. A sin forsaken is a sin forgiven when the thought or idea that prompted the sin is corrected. **(465)**

James explains the truth clearly in saying, "Every man is tempted, when he is drawn away of his own lust, and enticed. Then when lust hath conceived, it bringeth forth sin." Simply put, it means that every **(466)**

(467) man when he conceives an idea that is wrong, destructive, or evil, and dwells upon it, eventually causes it to become a fact. When he wishes to overcome a sinful condition he does not waste time wrestling with the fact, but corrects, forsakes, forgets, forgives the idea that started it. This is the weed in the garden that must be pulled out top, stock, root and all to be completely destroyed.

(468) At another time we find that Jesus repeated the Law and with some explanation. In His prayer He states, "Forgive us our debts as we forgive our debtors." This is a perfectly reasonable proposition. As we forgive those who transgress against us, so shall we be forgiven of our transgressions. This law has followed us down through time, and today we speak of it as though it were something new; we call it "modern psychology." The Law reads that certain ideas must be

(469) dissolved and cleared from the mind in order that other ideas or new ideas of a different character may replace them. It may be explained as a bottle that is already full which must be emptied before it can be refilled or added to. Jesus spoke of it when He said: "Neither do men put new wine in old bottles, else the bottles break."

(470) For example, if you hold in your mind that someone has wronged you or has treated you unjustly, you cannot be free from your wrongdoings or injustice so long as you hold that thought in your consciousness. Often people complain that they do not understand clearly or get the illumination of spirit as others have testified. You need only to search your memory to find

the cause. If you do not get the understanding you expect, first search your mind for lurking, unforgiving thoughts that have been tucked away from your notice. Is your thought realm filled with resentment that you may hold against some person or condition? Have you a feeling that you have been slighted by this person or that one? The Law reads, "If ye forgive not (471) their trespasses, neither will your Father forgive your trespasses." We make the conditions for ourselves as we meet the demands of the Law.

Some people ask if we believe in canceling monetary obligations of those who owe us, or, literally, (472) should we cancel the debts of our debtors? There were a number of people in the past months who have made the front page in the newspaper because they wrote off their books with receipts in full to all who owed them. Did this eliminate the debts? Well, the debtors were loud in their praises for such a generous soul, but they came right back to do more business with the grocer or the butcher and asked them to charge it. In other words, they were glad to be relieved of the debt charged against them, but they knew no different than to return and open a new account.

The answer is, that so long as we believe in the necessity and reality of debt, such debt will continue (473) to endure. So long as we believe in debts we shall get into debt and continue to collect all the burdens and headaches that come with them. He who does not in his own thought release all men who owe him stands liable, himself, to fall into debt. If we send receipted bills to all who owe us, would that relieve us from the burden of debt? No, the signing of the receipts does not erase the idea of debt from our minds. First we must erase from our minds the thought that anyone can owe us anything. This then will bring us into a clear atmosphere in which we sow seeds or ideas of abundance for those who are indebted to us. In this way the debtors will find their minds more fertile soil to bring forth thoughts of abundance. When they catch

(474) the spirit of the free flowing thought of plenty, they will be happy to pay their debts, and all that is justly ours will come to us cheerfully. In other words, when we free our minds from all thoughts of debt and try to realize more and more the presence of plenty, we shall soon be strong enough to reach out and realize abundance for our debtors. As they are lifted up from the

(475) thoughts of limitation and lack, they will attract more and more substance with which they can pay their bills. In this way, and only in this way, can debts be permanently canceled. Through applying the Law of Forgiveness both parties concerned will be lifted from a debt consciousness to a prosperous consciousness, and prosperity and plenty shall abound.

(476) Everyone must at some time walk the path of forgiveness. We must learn to live this Law. It must be important, for the Master taught that there was no hope of forgiveness for the unforgiving. Only as we

(477) forgive are we forgiven. We must put forth the first effort. Our willingness must open the way for our forgiveness. We dare not ask more of the Law than we are able to extend to ourselves or to our brothers. Unless we prove this Law by living it, we cannot hope

to gain the bigness of character that life requires.

As we ponder over this whole thought, we may wonder if the Master was looking forward to the essential part forgiveness must play in the order of the world events of today. The Truth runs deep into everyday life. When we recall the rivalries that prevail in almost every shop and office, when we see the jealousies that divide the neighborhood, when we observe and feel the envies both scholastic and professional, when we have strife and discord in our own homes, we see the solemn, though simple, teachings of forgiveness strike deeply into your life and mine. If we cannot forgive, we may know we have a small soul untouched by the teachings of the Master. These are our daily tests, for it is in the school of forgiveness that the lessons of life are learned.

(478)

(479)

Law of Forgiveness

FORGIVE

(480)

That slight misdeed of yesterday,
    why should it mar today?
The thing he said, the thing you did,
    have long since passed away;
For yesterday was but a trial;
    today you will succeed,
And from mistakes of yesterday
    will come some noble deed.

Forgive yourself for thoughtlessness,
    do not condemn the past;
For it is gone with its mistakes;
    their mem'ry cannot last;
Forget the failures and misdeeds,
    from such experience rise,
Why should you let your head be bowed?
    Lift up your heart and eyes!

— Selected

X

LAW OF SACRIFICE

"Strait is the gate, and narrow is the way, which leadeth unto life, and few there be that findeth it."
Matt. 7:14

EVERY MAN SHOULD HAVE AN IDEAL or a hero. If there is one who has none and desires none, do not trust him too far. A man who has no ideals does not wish to be any greater than he is, and will in time prove a detriment to others. Abraham Lincoln is the ideal hero for the American youth, and that applies to any youth from six to sixty or over. **(481)**

Lincoln came from the lowliest and poorest of stock and yet rose to the highest office in the land that we as a people can bestow. There is hardly a boy or a man today who cannot say that he has as many or more natural gifts and opportunities than Lincoln had. He was plain and honest and determined to get along in his world. He had many faults like all of us. He would rather rest his lanky body in some comfortable position and proceed to tell yarns than to do any work. He was neither as polite nor as polished as his wife wanted him to be. He had but a few dollars in his pocket when he moved into the White House as our President. But money does not make a man. Polished manners do not make him. Even education does not make great a man whose soul is small. **(482)**

Abe's soul began to grow from the seed of thought that was placed in his mind when yet a small lad by his mother, who made it a point to teach him what she could when she was able. One day Mrs. Lincoln became very ill, and, knowing that she was dying, called her family around her bedside, then placing her feeble hand upon little Abe's head she said to them, "Be good to one another." She expressed the hope that they live as she had taught them, loving their kindred and worshipping God. She had done her work and, stoop-shouldered, thin breasted, sad, at times most miserable, without prospect of better conditions on earth, she passed away. She may have dreamed, but little realized the grand future that lay in store for the ragged, hapless boy who stood at her side.

(483) Though Abe was quite young at her passing, he never forgot his mother. She taught him a lesson that he carried with him through life. She taught him that the beginning of wisdom is not imposed by discipline, but the beginning of wisdom is first the desire for discipline, the love of it, the voluntary choice of it. Thus he learned that discipline is the high road that leads to everything that makes life worth living.

(484) Go to a concert or opera today and listen to the voice that captivates the music lovers who hear it— voices of such artists as McCormick, Lily Pons, Thomas, Eddy, McDonald, Moore, and your favorites that you can name. How do they ever happen? Ah, they do not happen. Granted that they may be especially gifted, but those final magical results come not by chance or accident, but from discipline. Discipline that is consciously chosen, ardently desired, and patiently persisted in.

Law of Sacrifice

Yet we hear it said that we are an undisciplined generation of people. This, however, is not true. In every realm of life we enjoy the fruits of disciplined research and toil, with results far greater than our forefathers ever dreamed. I shall never forget the thrilling experience I had one evening sitting in my home before a cozy fireside. The radio was beside my chair and I casually reached over, turned it on, and selected a prominent station. To my keen surprise I heard a voice calling Richard Byrd in the Antarctic regions at the South Pole. I then heard the Commander tell of the hazards and difficulties they had met the day before as they unloaded supplies and hauled them to their new home, Little America, over the slope of broken ice and drifted snow. Had he written a detailed report and sent it by letter it would have taken months to reach us, yet here in less than a second his voice vibrated through the air and I, like many others, heard him report the happenings of the day. The old miracle workers never dreamed that such as this could happen. Happen—that is not the word; discipline—that is it. It was painstaking, scientific, technical discipline that produced such a result. (485)

We are not an undisciplined generation in any realm except one, and that is in our morals. In science, in art, in athletics, in any practical endeavor we know the worth of discipline. Yet we let ourselves go, we must have our fling, we unleash our instincts and throw off restraint. It is the denial of discipline that characterizes much of our moral life. Men everywhere are awakening to the necessity of disciplining their (486)

(487) thoughts and acts. We train domestic animals carefully, we harness the forces of Nature to serve us regularly and well, and yet when it comes to ourselves, the most valued of all, we let our thoughts run wild. No one can attain his ambitions until he learns to discipline his mental force and is able to control his think

(488) ing. No one can be truly religious before his mind is in order and his ideals are brought in harmony with the Divine mind. No one can gain wisdom and understanding of life except that he seeks it in God's appointed way according to the Law.

First let us note one simple fact. SOMETHING ALWAYS HAS TO BE SACRIFICED FOR SOMETHING ELSE. Everything in

(489) life has its own price and is ever up for sale. We have to purchase it at the price it demands. Day after day we go up to life's counter and say, "I will give you this if you will give me that." This bartering has another name more familiar perhaps; we call it "sacrifice." Sacrifice, then, is not what our preachers have made it out to be. It is an inescapable necessity. It is a definite law that we must obey. We are sacrificing every day of our lives whether we want to or not, whether we know it or not. No matter what we want of life we have to give up something in order to get it.

From one of the Master's sayings the modern mind shrinks back and tries to avoid. "Strait is the gate, and

(490) narrow is the way, which leadeth unto life, and few there are that findeth it." How we dislike to hear such words. We are through with narrowness, we say. We are more liberal today, we want the broad open ways. We claim our freedom and declare there is no need for

us to be so narrow. We will not go through the small and narrow way. Yet there are few statements that Jesus uttered that are more accurate and complete than that one. No man will ever find the richness of life in any realm by loose and casual wandering. Always he will have to go down a narrow way and through a strait gate called discipline.

Go hear Kreisler play his violin and listen to music that is almost divine. Watch the skilled surgeon at his delicate task of repairing a broken body that it may hold its life a little longer for the soul to grow stronger. Consider the scientist in his laboratory with his scientific formulas. (491)

Remember George Eliot saying that she was a young woman when she began *Romola* but an old one when she finished it. Or think of Admiral Byrd flying over the South Pole and talking to us about it by means of radio. Are such experiences life? Indeed they are. Liberated life of an attained achievement, the most satisfying sort of living man can ever know, but strait is the gate and narrow is the way of discipline that leads to such a life.

When this law of sacrifice is carried over into the moral realm, it is commonly presented one-sided. We are taught that if we want to live a good life we have to give up so many pleasures. How familiar that sounds to some of us. The result is that we rebel, and when we think of sacrifice we think of the ones who have had to give up so much pleasure for goodness. Who are some of the great sacrificers in history? Well, there was Socrates who drank the hemlock; there was (492)

Jesus who was crucified on the cross; there was Paul who was beheaded; there was Peter who was crucified upside down; there were Luther and Wesley and Calvin, all religionists; there were Livingstone, Nightingale and scores of others. But think for a moment, are they the ones who made the most terrific sacrifices?

(493) We speak of the supreme sacrifice of Jesus upon the cross; we read of the martyrdom of Saints Peter, Paul, and John but what about Judas Iscariot? Think of what he had a chance to become. Think of the companionship he once possessed, and the place he might have occupied. Think of what he threw away. Think of what he got for it. I say to you, the Cross was not a sacrifice to be compared with what Judas paid. For but thirty pieces of silver and utter disgrace he cast aside the richest opportunity of any man in all history. A youth who had disdained discipline, had cast aside restraint and had his fling wrote as he sat behind (494) prison bars, "A thousand, thousand times I have paid in full for those few hours." This young man and his nephew, a few years his junior, had attended a revival meeting in a town not far from me, and on their way home they argued the question the minister had talked about at the meeting. The argument grew into angry words, and when they reached home this anger had been fanned to a murderous heat. The younger man went to his room, and got a gun, and shot at the uncle. The uncle in turn wrestled for the gun and turned it upon the youth and killed him. I say this is costly living. We should take this earnestly unto our-

selves and realize how the word sacrifice touches every one of us.

A man called at my office seeking help in a very serious problem. He had a fine home, a lovely, devoted wife, and two splendid children. It is true that the (495) wife had taken up much of her time with the children and the husband was going out to his club and social affairs alone. He had met another woman and thought he was in love with her. This was his problem, what about the family and the home? There is only one answer, and it is not for me or any mortal to decide. The Law will determine it for you. You cannot have a lovely home, a devoted family and enjoy loose living. (496) If you will not sacrifice or give up the loose living for the lovely home, you will be forced to sacrifice a lovely home and loved ones for loose living. You cannot enjoy the satisfactions and pleasures of a true friendship and indulge in a bad temper. If you will not sacrifice your temper for friendships, you will sacrifice (497) your friendships for a bad temper. One cannot have a sterling character that friends will respect and trust and resort to crooked practices. If he will not give up his crooked ways for trustworthiness, he will have to sacrifice his trustworthiness for crookedness.

You may ever be sure of this: no matter how far you may go before the rope gets tight, no matter how (498) wild or how lax you may live, even though you think you are getting away with it and do, you cannot fool the Law. Something always has to be paid for something else. All fine living, all success and happiness is like fine art; you must choose the spiritual beauty to be

Law of Sacrifice

created and desired, then go the strait and narrow way to gain it. For, the beginning of wisdom is first the desire of discipline.

(499) Some say then that if you want to enjoy the pleasures of life, this means that your freedom is impossible. It means on the contrary that you, who think this, have not found what real freedom is. This reminds me of a drunkard who was giving a stump lecture to the amusement of a few on the subject of freedom. He declared he wanted his freedom and that he had a right to drink all the liquor he wanted and no government could stop him. He was having his freedom and yet he was so drunk he did not know what he was saying or doing. Freedom is not living an obsessed, undisciplined life. Freedom is in being able to control your life and in making it what you want it to be.

(500) If you wish to become a skilled athlete, an efficient teacher, an expert lawyer, or a beautiful singer, the beginning of such success is first the desire for discipline of your time and thought. If you want that rich, radiant, and worthwhile specialty in living life, the rule is just the same. AN UNDISCIPLINED LIFE IS AN INSANE LIFE. We must pull ourselves together around high ideals of clean, serviceable, and effective living under

(501) the highest leadership we know, or under the teachings and the example of a master.

(502) The highest example of a master is the Christ. In all His work and teachings He proved that discipline, self-control, and self-mastery ever precede wisdom and achievement. Mrs. Lincoln had taught His words to little Abe, and it was because Abe grew into man-

hood and sacrificed his life of laziness, looseness, and careless meanderings for the strait and narrow way of a disciplined life of principle and honesty and justice that caused him to become a great soul. It was the law of sacrifice working through him that enabled him to become the President and Savior of a great Nation.

Evidence of this greatness was seen in his work at Washington. During the war a young Vermont boy, whose name was William Scott, was sentenced to face (503) the firing squad for being found asleep at his post. Now it wasn't Scott's post but that of his buddy whom he had relieved when he became ill. Double duty was too much for Scott, so he fell asleep. He was so well liked by all that his captain and friends appealed his case to the President. Lincoln decided to go to Chain Bridge and handle the case in person. He went to the camp and talked to Scott. Scott said he was the kindest person he had ever met. He said the President had asked him about his home, the farm, his friends, and lastly his mother. He said he was glad he could draw a picture of her out of the bosom of his shirt and show it to him. Mr. Lincoln told him how thankful he should be to have a mother and how he should make her a proud mother and that he should never cause her another sorrow or tear. Scott thought it very strange that he did not speak of his fate in the morning. Strange that he should advise not to cause his mother another sorrow or tear when he was about to die. Finally he mustered up his courage and asked the President if he would grant one favor, namely, that he would not have to face his friends, but that a firing

Law of Sacrifice

squad be drawn from another company. Mr. Lincoln wheeled about, and facing Scott said, "My boy, you are not going to be shot tomorrow. I am going to trust you and send you back to your friends. As I have been put to considerable trouble to come up from Washington, how are you going to pay the bill?"

The boy stammered his gratitude; he suggested he could send him his savings; he could borrow money by mortgaging the farm; his friends would help, too, and there was all his army pay. Then Mr. Lincoln put his hands on the boy's shoulders, and looking sorrowfully into his face, he said, "My boy, my bill is a very large one; your friends cannot pay it, nor your bounty, nor the farm, nor your comrades. There is only one man in all this world who can pay it, and his name is William Scott. If from this day William Scott does his duty so that if I were to be there when he comes to die, he can look me in the face as he is now doing and say, 'I have kept my promise,' then my debt will be fully paid."

(504) William Scott kept that promise. He had learned the secret that Mr. Lincoln's mother had taught him when a boy. It was this law of sacrifice, and that the beginning of such wisdom was first the desire and love of discipline; that it was the strait and narrow way that led to the high road of everything that makes life worth living. It was the road that led Mr. Lincoln to the White House. It was the road that leads back to the Vermont hills, to home, to happiness, and to mother. It is the road for all who persevere and find it. It is the road that Jesus followed to triumph and mastery.

Law of Sacrifice

It is the road I recommend to you, for on it you will find the Law of Sacrifice ever working to bring to you the joys and the pleasures that result always from the wisdom and understanding that accompany it.

(505)

"Blessed is the man who endureth temptation, for when he is tried he shall receive the crown of life, which the Lord (Law) has promised to them that love him."

INVICTUS

Out of the night that covers me,
    Black as the pit from pole to pole,
I thank whatever gods may be
    For my unconquerable soul.

(506)

In the fell clutch of circumstance
    I have not winced nor cried aloud.
Under the bludgeonings of Chance
    My head is bloody, but unbowed.

Beyond this place of wrath and tears
    Looms but the horror of the shade,
And yet this menace of the years
    Finds, and shall find me unafraid.

It matters not how straight the gate,
    How charged with punishment the scroll.
I am the master of my fate;
    I am the captain of my soul.

—W. E. Henley

XI

LAW OF OBEDIENCE

"Obey my voice, and I will be your God, and ye shall be my people."

Jer. 7:23

TO BE USHERED INTO TURMOIL, blindly toil a few years and then go out into uncertainty, is surely not the purpose of Man's existence. Life must mean more than this, and it does mean more. Man should be a builder, and to him is given all the materials out of which to construct the kind of life he desires to live. He builds in wisdom or in ignorance, according to his obedience, according to his understanding of a Divine Law and the use of it in his daily life. (507)

Many people, when they learn that the science of living is governed by exacting laws, immediately assume that to live rightly is to live the hard way. They are afraid of a law that is exacting in its demands when it touches their relationship with the finer things. Yet these same people would not be willing that the laws which govern human society should be modified in any way. They recognize that the laws which govern social conduct and activity must be properly enforced if organized society is to function harmoniously and safely. In other words, they recognize that government is for the good of mankind and that without it human life and welfare would be in continual jeopardy. (508) (509)

(510) If this is true of human government and established by constitution and law, it is even more true of divine government. And the more exacting the law, the more certain the safety, prosperity, and happiness of him who fulfills the law's demands. In the realm of science no laws are more exacting than those which govern the science of mathematics. An accountant, even when he fails immediately to solve a problem, knows it can be solved only by calling into operation the exacting laws that govern all mathematical calcu-

(511) lations. Were those laws subject to change, the solution of mathematical problems would be utterly hopeless.

Perhaps in no way has religion gone so far astray as in its conception or understanding of God, whether it be the God of the Christians or of the heathen.

(512) Instead of recognizing that the Supreme Intelligence is Law, operating according to and as surely as the Laws of Nature, men have created in their ideas a God who is partial, subject to appeal from saint and sinner alike; a God who can be persuaded and bargained with; a God who gives life and takes it away; a God who heals sickness and causes it; a God who impoverishes and enriches; a God who rewards and punishes; and having accepted this wrong idea, it has made prayer largely a matter of doubts, lacking in that strong assurance that a thing will be so because it is according to the Divine Law.

To many folks this aspect of truth creates an illusion of a God for all; a God who is not interested in man's needs and problems; a God who is not a father to whom we can take our cares and with whom we can converse. "They have taken away my Lord," cried Mary. Sooner or later, however, they discover that this divine knowledge of the nature of God, as Law, has (513) given them their Lord in a sense so close and intimate that all doubt in claiming their good is ended; for once the Law is understood, we hold the secret of eternal happiness, peace, and dominion or mastery over all the forces around us.

The word "obey" means to submit to rule or to comply with orders or instructions. Obedience, then, is the governor of all movement whether it be mechanical, literal, or spiritual. A giant machine without its (514) governor would tear itself apart, would be utterly destroyed because it failed to obey its own laws of momentum or gravity. An intellectual giant who fails to comply with the laws of learning will become as an idiot. A student failing to comply with or to obey the instructions of spirit, the Law of God, will reverse that good and create evil. We are dependent entirely on obedience for our success or failure in this life.

Our societies, cities, states and nation are supported by it. Our properties and lives are dependent upon it. Because of our respect for obedience, we, as a whole, support it. But woe unto the man who tries to break through to pillage, to plunder for selfish gain. As we look into the home we see the mother training (515) her child into habits of discipline. Tomorrow we see a happy mother because her child has grown into youth and manhood and has earned success. A success because, back in the beginning of his life, the seed of (516)

159

(517) obedience was placed there which brought forth respect, obedience, and unselfish thought. On the other hand, we may see where others fail because they have been allowed to grow up being disobedient, disrespectful, and selfish.

(518) Business is founded upon obedience, and as each member obeys the laws of commerce, he will succeed. It is only when man expands these laws by over-speculation, and by wild-cat schemes, inflated values, or lack of cooperative agency, that he brings upon himself failures and causes bankruptcies and loss. All our problems of life are due in some measure to our obedience to the Law of Thought and its Creator, God.

(519) Our difficulties have been in knowing what to obey and what not to obey.

(520) We see in Nature the answer. She has no troubles she cannot overcome. She has no problems she cannot solve. She has no burdens she cannot bear; no tasks she cannot perform. Why?

(521) All her operations are governed by the mighty Law of Harmony and Order which constantly removes every discord, which heals all diseases, which rights every wrong, which supplies every need. If, in the winter, a young sprout attempts to break through the soil before season, Mother Nature destroys that sprout, rills it off or freezes it out. Yet, at the same time, the very snow and ice that freeze the little unruly sprout, serve as a blanket of warmth and protection to the other seedlings complying with her

(522) laws. When man wishes to use Nature in his work, such as farming or gardening, he must know how to

Law of Obedience

comply with Nature's law. In turn, as he obeys her laws, he derives the best results, and in the end he will enjoy the greatest harvest. He who obeys the laws of Nature and acts as her obedient servant, later becomes (523) the master and reaps a full harvest.

Every student who obeys the Law and is a true servant of Good will become a greater soul and will reap the power to control his every condition and enjoy blessings galore. This is what the Master tried to tell us (524) when he said, "He that is greatest among you shall be your servant; whosoever shall exalt himself shall be humbled; whosoever shall humble himself shall be exalted." Yet this does not picture for us a weakling, one who gives way to the stronger or is easily brushed aside by the more aggressive, for Paul says, "When I am weak, I am strong," meaning, of course, that when he is weak to obey the Law of Good, he is strong and spirited.

Our mistakes are largely due to the fact that we have obeyed more readily the laws of earth than the (525) Laws of Spirit. We have subjected our ideas to the outward appearances of things rather than to the inner truths as the Law teaches them. Peter and the apostles said to those who gathered about them in the marketplace, "We must obey God rather than man." We must obey the Law of Good rather than the law of man. They knew that an individual is only as he thinks he is, and if he obeys the promptings of the Spirit or the (526) urge of his senses, his results will be accordingly. Paul says, "Know ye not to whom ye yield yourselves servants to obey, his servants ye are to whom ye obey;

whether of sin unto death or obedience unto righteousness."

(527)   If we are to obey the Spirit within us rather than
the conditions about us, then the Law requires us to
first think things into existence from the within before
we shall see them on the without. Most of our experiences are the outgrowth of our own created activities.
These created activities are first to be bound in
thought that we think in our minds. The law reads,
(528)   "As ye sow, so shall ye reap," which is mathematically
accurate and true. If you plant a turnip seed, Nature
does not produce potatoes. If you plant a corn seed,
Nature does not make a mistake and bring forth a
giant oak tree. On the same reasoning, if you plant
thoughts of worry, the law you obey will give you
(529)   something to worry about. It will produce more and
more circumstances to increase your worries. If you
think of disease and lack, you will receive exactly
what you are expecting. Whatever law you obey will
in turn serve you. The most important thing then is to
know what to obey.

You laugh at the troubles of little ones because you
(530)   view them from their true value. To the child his tiny
task seems real and all important, and not until he out-
grows his childish ways can he look back with amusement and not feel regret. Not until we can rise superi-
or to our problems and our troubles can we ever hope
to cease to have further troubles. A mother put her little boy to bed one night, but later she found him rest-
less, unable to sleep. He called down and asked that
(531)   the light be left lighted for him. The mother knew

something was wrong so she went up to his room and gained his confidence by talking with him. She learned that during the day other children had threatened to send the "boogie man" after him because he would not give over his toy to them. The mother then explained that there was no "boogie man." She said that the principle of it was to frighten him into submission so that he would give over his toy to the other children. She told him he could go to sleep because there was no real "boogie man." The child had obeyed the illusion of things and was frightened, but the mother saw the truth. In knowing the truth she could see through the principle of fear involved, and by dispelling it from the mind of her son, enable him to go peacefully to sleep. (532)

The purpose of our lesson is to learn how we might properly choose and serve the Law for our highest good. We either serve principle or things in all that we think and do. Things are the events or the results of invisible causes, whereas principle is the true cause and is spirit. Principle is that which we think in our minds and things are the results of those thoughts. A man who obeys illusions or worships things, will have burdens to carry. A man's burdens are the things which he claims as his personal property. Things that he feels are his very own and, therefore, he must protect and serve them. Years ago a relative of mine worshipped illusions and things. He strove to accumulate riches. He worked so hard gaining his wealth that he lost his health. Then he turned about and tried to gain his health by spending his wealth, (535)

(533)

(534)

and in the end he passed away, a disappointed and disillusioned man. That man, like so many others, had started out in life with the wrong conception of the Law of God.

Strange, but man does not own an earthly thing. All that he has has been loaned to him according to his

(536) understanding of the law he serves. Man was born naked and he dies in that nakedness. All his earthly things are stripped off of him; even his many burdens become illusions again. His real task in life is to find

(537) his place according to his understanding, and that understanding determines the way he lives life. Analyze your burdens. They arise from some ideas of possession that you think. You may have dependents,

(538) others who must be supplied, and you feel you must care for them, as they have no other protector or provider. But when you realize the allness of God, who sees even the sparrows fall, you will then change

(539) your idea of responsibility. Then your mental release will permit a greater flow of good to come to you, and it will come to you in many other ways than before. Thousands today are held in bondage to the idea that they must be helped by others, that they must have

(540) relief. Their greatest need is not your help or mine so much as it is a new understanding of life itself. The fear of the future has become a race belief and it affects all ages. As you obey the law of fear instead of the Law of God, you will have many more burdens. For only as we are able to cast our burdens upon the Law shall we be free.

If you are obedient to the Law you will not suffer these burdens to be heaped high upon you. You will live in the present, do your highest duty every day, forget the past, and let the future take care of itself. For to trust the Law you must know of its guidance by experience and practice. To those who have not learned this guidance, the experience must be acquired. God does not require you to follow his leading on blind trust. Behold the evidence of an invisible intelligence pervading everything, even your own mind and body.

(541)

Disobedience to the Law is refusal to do what we know is right. We all know the right, but we do not always do it because it seems to interfere or delay our immediate attainment of the object we see. We want quick returns, forgetting that the Law moves slowly, yet it works perfectly and well. We want instantaneous healing of our diseases, but we are loath to give up the net of habits that caused them.

(542)

When we speak of a man of principle we mean a man who is governed by the law of right thinking and living; a man who is not easily swayed; a man who is not an opportunist; a man who will not deviate from the path of what he deems to be right for the sake of personal profit or popular acclaim; a man, in short, whom one may trust absolutely to be true to his convictions regardless of the temptations to change or modify them. No one will deny that such a man inspires the utmost confidence and may become a tower of strength and leadership. He is one on whom

(543)

165

others rely for leadership, whereas the man who is easily persuaded to yield to pressure, even for kindly motives, is not the type of individual on whom we can depend.

(544) If this is true of man in the outer realm, how much more true it is of man in the inner realm, the mental realm, because God is Principle — not merely governed by principle. The God-governed man is never in doubt as to the results to be gained by following the principle, for principle is based on law and obedience. So this Law can have only one result: happiness, peace, and prosperity.

(545) All that is required of us is to learn obedience to the Law of Truth and not to obey the petty things that arise steadily as we allow our visions to be disturbed and harassed. Blessed are they that hear the word of God and keep it. "Obey my voice and I will be your God and ye shall be my people." When we obey the voice (Law), then we understand with the Master the statement, "All that is mine is thine." This is the Law acting through us. As we obey the Law, we humble our personal self to the Divine self within us. We (546) refuse to accept the outer appearances of things as being final and true but we turn within and seek that which is real and true as God, the Law, intended it to be. Let us live with God in His work, not after we die, not tomorrow or next year, but right here and now. God's kingdom is all about us, awaiting our acknowledgment or obedience of His Law. We must be able to converse and live with God, the Law, in our daily life. Then we shall live with love and joy, with hope and

wealth and peace here and everywhere. It is ours for the decision.

"If they obey and serve Him, they shall spend their days in prosperity and their years in pleasure."

Job 36:11.

RESOLVE

Build on resolve, and not upon regret,
  The structure of the future. Do not grope
(547) Among the shadows of old sins, but let
  Thine own soul's light shine on the path of hope,

And dissipate the darkness. Waste no tears
  Upon the blotted record of lost years,
But turn the leaf and smile, oh smile to see
  The fair white pages that remain for thee.

Prate not thy repentance. But believe
  That spark divine dwells in thee: let it grow.
That which the upreaching spirit can achieve
  The grand and all-creative forces know;
They will assist and strengthen as the light
  Lifts up the acorn to the oak tree's height.
Thou hast but to resolve, and lo! God's whole
  Great universe shall fortify thy soul.

— *Ella Wheeler Wilcox*

XII

LAW OF SUCCESS

"He can who thinks he can."

GOD INTENDED every individual to succeed. It is God's purpose that man should become great. It is God's will **(548)** that man should not only use, but enjoy, every good in the universe. The Law of God denies man nothing.

Man is born to be rich. The powers inherent in him are inexhaustible. Each normal person is endowed **(549)** with a complete set of faculties which, if properly developed and scientifically applied, will insure success, ever-growing success.

Man is made for progress. Every man contains within himself the capacity for endless development. Advancement into all things is the Law's great pur- **(550)** pose. By learning to work with the Law in promoting that aim, man may build himself into greater and greater success.

All the processes of Nature are successful. Nature knows no failures. She never plans anything but suc- **(551)** cess. She aims at results in every form and manner. To succeed in the best and fullest sense of the term we must, with Nature as our model, copy her methods. In her principles and laws we shall discover all the secrets of success.

(552) Infinite resources are at man's disposal. There are no limits to his possibilities. He focuses and individualizes the elements, forces, and principles of the whole world. He can develop a wonderful intelligence; thus, all life's questions may be answered, all Nature's secrets discovered, and all human problems solved. Nothing is impossible.

(553) Higher faculties, remarkable talents, superior insight, and greater power are dormant in all, and by special psychological methods, these exceptional elements can be developed to an extraordinary degree for actual and practical use. Every mind can develop greatness. It is simply a matter of knowing how. True self-help, self-discovery, self-knowledge, and the proper instruction in applying one's faculties and using one's forces will advance any person. Practice will insure efficiency; use will bring forth results. Success, therefore, is within the reach of every aspiring man.

(554) Do you wish to succeed? You can. You possess all the essentials within yourself; all you need is to gain a right understanding of the principles and laws upon which success is based, and then to apply the right methods of operating these causes until success is earned.

(555) The law of success is as definite as the laws of any science. The exact use of this law will produce results every time. It is results that count; and as results may be multiplied indefinitely by a persistent application of this law, there is no ending to the success you can enjoy. Great things are no less possible than small

Law of Success

things, and it is the great things that will follow who-
ever uses the law with faith and understanding.
Whatever your present state or condition may be,
there is a better and a larger future in store for you, but
you must prepare yourself for it. You cannot rise into   (556)
the better and greater things unless you Do SOMETHING
about it. Study, planning, and effort are all necessary.
The young and the old alike are entitled to advance.
To be true to yourself and to the Law which governs
you, you simply must advance, for advancement is
success. It is the Law's intention that you shall move
forward. You can stand still, and you can go back-   (557)
ward, thus retarding your normal progress for a
while, perhaps as long as a lifetime, but in the end you
will be compelled to move forward, especially in the
direction of soul's growth.

Nature brooks no interferences with her purposes.   (558)
This is often the reason why "prods and pricks" of
adversity come when you fail to move forward. There
is a new element abroad, the spirit of progress, and we
must all keep pace with the times.

You can achieve your ambition. Aim high and
build well. What you imagine to yourself as success   (559)
can be reached. The Law never blunders; what she
idealizes, she has the power to actualize; what she
images in your mind, she has the power to produce
materially. She ever seeks to build you up in your
power and in success; that is her plan for you. The faculties possessed by all great and successful men are   (560)
the same human faculties you possess. They gained
some understanding of the right kind, and then they

171

applied their faculties in the best way they knew for advancement, and so earned success. Some will ask, "But in what does true success consist?" Almost every other person will hold a different view as to what constitutes real success. To avoid confusion of ideas, let us define our meaning of the term. Most people consider **(561)** success as being a high state of worldly prosperity; others, as the realization of personal hopes, or fulfillment of heart's desires; still others, as the achievement of their ambitions or the performance of great deeds. Real success, however, is something more than this. We do not define it in terms of money, position, fame or wealth, although it may include all these. True, genuine success of the largest kind lies in the results obtained, harvest reaped and distributed, so that our fellow beings at large are benefited and the world enriched. Yet for the purpose of our lesson, the term success will be interpreted in a more individual sense as meaning personal advancement and increase, and the favorable termination of anything attempted.

(562) Man is so constructed that he may utilize the elements of his life to build himself up into an ever-increasing power, betterment and success. He is also subtly related to everything outside of himself that this purpose may be fulfilled. Such fulfillment, however, will depend on the actual use he makes of his **(563)** mind, and whether he chooses to serve in ignorance or to govern with knowledge the forces in his life.

(564) Success is bringing one's self and one's actions to a standard higher than the ordinary human standard. Most all the failures and defeats in life are due to mental blindness. When the heart is right the head thinks right. All our acts are judged by our inner motives, not by the outer accomplishments. "Out of the heart are the issues of life." Moral cowardice, indecision at criti- (565) cal moments, a desire to have one's own way, inability to cooperate, have shattered the hopes of millions. They have wrecked their prospects of success. To eliminate these mental handicaps is the first move for all who wish to aim high.

Success depends upon adopting a true course, upholding what is just and right in thought and action. Adherence to a principle is most essential. Success is not a creature of circumstance, nor a game (566) of chance, nor luck, for not until the Golden Rule is the basis of commercial activity can we be in harmony with the principle. Religion and business are not two separate sciences; they are both as one. Lord Leverhulme said, "It is frequently stated that modern business cannot be conducted on the line of the (567) Sermon on the Mount. I can only say that a business conducted on any other basis will never be permanently successful." Business is an expression of man's highest aim, man's religion.

The fact that a man is honest and truthful and industrious does not insure his success. More may be (568) necessary than this, for if a man is timid, backward, or fearful, fear will act as a brake to retard his progress. If a man is an efficient engineer, yet has an inferiority complex, that complex will make him mediocre and he will not be able to extend himself according to his skillful training. Fear is largely the cause of failures; it cannot be eliminated either by drugs or by the surgeon's knife. The only remedy known for fear is understanding. When one understands that the universe is filled with the presence of God, there is nothing to fear.

(569) Most of us could meet our obligations if it were not for fear of some kind that tells us differently. We hypnotize ourselves into a belief which incapacitates our power. Fear clouds our vision, it benumbs our faculties, it paralyzes our mental forces which must be free and active if we are to avert calamity. When man's mind is confused by fear, he is in no condition to accept an opportunity. "God does not give us the spirit of fear, but of courage and a sound mind."

(570) Man's religion does not make for him a success. If a man wears glasses to improve his vision, for the same reason man gets more out of life with a religion that serves to enlarge his vision. A true religion serves to expand or to enlarge man's vision, whereas the practical irreligious man is cramped by his narrow and limited view. If we think supply depends upon people or material conditions and then are worried when people fail us, conditions go from bad to worse. The only safeguard is to feel and know that God (the Law) is our supply, and to affirm it constantly. If we desire success, we must think success, we must talk (571) and act success, and we can do this more easily if we know that God, the Law, is on our side. "No good thing will God, the law, withhold from them that walk uprightly." The religious-minded man realizes that He that is for us is greater than that which is against us.

It is said that half our failures are a result of our pulling up on our horses and checking them as they are about to leap the barrier. Expert riders let the horse have his head and this insures a safe jump. Half our failures then are that we pull in at the moment when we should let all our forces out to have full vent as we make a leap. We jerk ourselves back into failure just when we could be riding on to victory. Two boys dove into the river one day, challenging one another to swim across, a distance of about two miles. They swam on with a strong and steady stroke and the lead swimmer, not looking back, continued swimming on toward the other shore. When he walked out on the bank of the river and had completed his swim, he looked back to note that his friend was nowhere near. He looked more carefully and, behold, there he stood back on the other shore from where they had started. When he met his friend he said to him, "How was it that you did not follow me across the stream and reach the other shore?" The boy who turned back said: "Oh, after I got about half way out I looked back and saw how far I had come and I was afraid I couldn't make it, so I turned back." "But," said the boy who swam across the stream, "why didn't you think to look forward as I did, for I saw only the shore corning closer and closer to me with each stroke. Why didn't you think it was just as hard to turn back to safety as it was to continue swimming to your goal?"

When Moses led the Children of Israel out of Egypt to the Promised Land, they met with what seemed to be an impossible barrier, the Red Sea. Some

(572)

(573)

(574)

175

wanted to turn back; many murmured and complained because they had ventured so far from Egypt. Moses cried out: "God, what shall I do?" and word came back to him, "Why criest thou unto me? Speak to thy children that they go forward." Moses spoke to his people, and as they marched into the sea the waters parted and they crossed over on dry land. Moses burned his bridges behind him as he went, then there could be no retreat.

(575) Success is a matter of advancement by grade. No man can become a success except by training. An athlete will train for weeks and months to fit himself for a contest that may last for only a few minutes. The real secret consists in moving forward, and that peculiar mental attitude which promotes this constant progress is the ruling factor in the art of success. No person can succeed who is not imbued with the desire to advance. In fact the first step is to become thoroughly saturated (576) with the "spirit of progress" so one feels stimulated with a persistent desire to work for better and greater things. The desire to advance implies the power to advance. That is the Law as absolute in its actions as any law of science. The fact that you desire to succeed (577) is evidence that you have the power to succeed; otherwise you would not have been urged to aspire successward. You cannot aspire to succeed unless you have the power to succeed. Desire creates the power; (578) power inspires the mind of the individual, and success is the result of that inspiration rightly applied.

Investigating the lives of successful men, we find a very striking fact: We find a common quality that is

responsible for their success, which consists of a constructive state of mind. Psychologists term this constructive state of mind as a "successful attitude." (579)
Simple as it may seem, in most every case the difference which decides success or failure is the ruling (580)
mental attitude. It is at fault and is the cause of failure. The discovery of this remarkable fact by modern psychology probes to the very root of some deep practicable problems and indicates a way out of adversity and failure. In short, the positive mental attitude of the man who thinks he CAN in contrast with the negative (581)
attitude of another who thinks he CAN'T, is practically the only difference between the one who succeeds and the one who fails. The former learns the truth and discovers he can do things and the idea liberates his sleeping energies, stirs them into activity, thrills him (582)
with the desire to advance, inspires him to get things done, so he moves into success.

Some persons, however, live in the conviction that as they are, so they must remain. They believe that (583)
God had cast them into a fixed mould and that the little ability or power which they possess is all they can hope or wish for in this life. Scientific research into the mysteries of the human mind reveals a wonderful world of power and possibility. The psychological truth is, that what is possible to one mind is possible (584)
to another, and vastly more than we have ever dreamed. The same human faculties and cultivated powers of the great and the successful are possible in all minds. The only real difference is in the degree of development, not kind.

Law of Success

(585) Begin now to take a superior view of yourself, your life and circumstances, and of things and persons in general. As you mentally perceive the better and greater, you will consciously and unconsciously reach out for the better and the greater. In other words, your thoughts, desires, words, and mental actions will gradually become filled with the "spirit of progress" and your faculties will grow stronger and your powers will increase.

(586) Catch the spirit of the words "I can" and you have the key to the successful attitude. Know you can succeed, and proceed to think, live, and act in that strong conviction. You may search everywhere, anywhere, to discover the mystic secret of success, only to find that in the end it is all contained in these two little words, "I can."

(587) Modern psychology has discovered that the person who thinks he can will speedily develop the power that can. This is a demonstrable law of the mind. Persistently think you can do what you want to do, and it will not be long before you find yourself actually doing that thing. There is no miracle about it; the law works that way. The principle involved is that if the "I can" attitude is adopted, the mind will proceed to direct all energies into those faculties which are employed in doing that which it is desired to accomplish, and steadily build them up until they become large enough and strong enough actually to perform what previously appeared to be impossible.

When Napoleon sought to conquer Italy he was faced with an apparently insurmountable obstacle, the towering Alps. They were considered by the people (588) who lived around them to be absolutely unscalable, but the words "I can't" were not in Napoleon's mind. He, being determined to conquer, persistently said to himself, "I can." His descent on the other side of the mountains so surprised the people in that country that they were practically conquered without opposition. The shock of his doing what was deemed impossible, took away their power of opposition. Thus, his greatest obstacle proved his sure means to victory. So it is with all difficulties. Obstacles viewed from a higher (589) point of view are invariably stepping stones to success. John Bunyan was thrown into prison, and while imprisoned there he faced a problem equal to the Alps. He wanted to continue with his religious work. He was not easily defeated, so on the twisted paper that was brought to him as a cork in the milk jug, he wrote his immortal "Pilgrim's Progress." This book alone has reached more people than he could have ever preached to in a whole lifetime.

Obstacles serve as an opportunity to call up our latent powers. They draw us out and make us strong; they lead us to the goal we have in view. When you (590) are up against it, when you desire to progress, declare to yourself these words, "I can." Remember those simple words contain the magic formula to all success and no goal worthwhile has ever been won without the realization of them.

One's state in life is largely determined by one's mental attitude. Men radiate discouragement, gloom, (591) and failure because they accept the "I can't" attitude.

Law of Success

Others positively emanate success through a cheerful confident, energetic "I can" attitude. We meet them everywhere. One gravitates to conditions of adversity, ill luck and misfortune; the other attracts the very best and rises on and on to success. The negative weak one, the "I can't" individual, repels us; we instinctively shun him; that is the Law warning us to avoid him because he is out of tune with the Divine order of things. On the other hand, the strong type of "I can" individual attracts and draws us to him. He is optimistic and we are glad to associate with and to do business with him. Everyone has his own individual **(592)** atmosphere, the same as a flower has its aroma. So let us seek to build up a strong positive "I can" attitude which will lead us to success.

In all circumstances you are greater than the things or the conditions; if not actually, you are potentially. **(593)** Whatever you aim at, be certain of winning; aim high, aim well, and your mistakes will come few and far between. Keep the "I can" attitude; affirm it constantly. You will succeed; you are bound to win. John P. Rockefeller states, "The man who starts out with the idea of getting rich won't succeed. He must have a **(594)** larger ambition. There is no mystery to business success. If he does each day's task successfully, stays faithfully within natural operations of commercial law, and keeps his head clear, he will come out all right."

The next step is to encompass your life or to state your ideal or your objective. Make a mental picture **(595)** and hold in mind that which you are aspiring to achieve. Begin with a persistent effort to work towards the final goal. Life, after all, is just like a series of many steps; each step may provide you with new problems, but as you meet each new problem, keep your eye ever fixed upon the top – your objective, your aim, your goal. No matter how crude or how poor your first efforts may be, they are but the beginning. You may not compare yourself with another; everyone has had to commence at some time at the very bottom. In the meantime, know that you cannot fail until you give up. You never can fail if you never give up. Keep on trying; each effort produces some result. Success, after all, is only the collection of many good results. (596) (597)

"Never leave till tomorrow that which you can do today," said Benjamin Franklin. The worst enemy you will encounter on life's highway is within your own self. Its name is PROCRASTINATION. Procrastination kills ambition. It gets one into the habit of indecision, which causes failure. Practice making your decisions clearly and promptly; take care of the little questions that come to you and they will automatically take care of any other big questions, should they arise. One who cannot decide for himself clearly subordinates his judgment; he becomes receptive to the racial thought around him and then he becomes one of the masses and can attract only what the masses supply. (598) (599)

What do you do with your spare time? How do you spend it? Where do you spend it? Do you give it any value? In these days much profit and sometimes the whole success depends upon the using of the odds and ends, the so-called "by-products." By-products are (600)

Law of Success

(601) something apart from the main article manufactured, and yet they have a value of their very own. All types of big business have their by-products, odds and ends, that pay them well. The Armour Meat Packing Company uses all their by-products to advantage. From the pigtails to the hair there are endless by-products. The pigtails are dried and sold as a delicacy; the hair is made into brushes and strong rope. Now if Armour neglected to use the by-products, there would be a great difference in the amount of dividends they pay their stockholders.

(602) The point for us is this: we may not be manufacturers like the Armour Meat Packing Company. We are dealers in time. Our success depends upon the use of our time and its many by-products which we call "odd moments." What about those odd moments? The real success of some started in the odd moments. What one does with his spare time, not only is clear profit, but it increases his mental activities. Every minute you save by making it useful and profitable, adds to your life and the possibility of a successful one. Every minute lost is a neglected by-product. Once it is gone it can never be returned.

(603) Think of the quarter-hour before breakfast, the half-hour after, and twenty minutes on the trolley, the time wasted awaiting appointments during the day, and the scores of chances each day when you might read, or figure, or concentrate, or work for your goal. Use all your time constructively. It is only the aimless, worthless, unsuccessful ones who speak of killing time. The one who is killing time is destroying his

opportunities, while the man who is succeeding is making his time live and making it useful. I always like to hear a person say that there isn't enough time in the day for him. That person is getting the most out of his life, and, I venture to say, he is succeeding.

Success, then, summarized, is the way we learn to use two valuable things – our time and thought. (604) Knowledge alone is not success; it is the way we use that knowledge. It is important always to remember that back of all our toil and struggle, under the dust and smoke of things, there are the arms of the Father guiding, guarding and supporting us. Whatever you lack, He has; whatever you need, He can supply; (605) whatever obstacle you encounter, God, within you and about you, can overcome it. "So near to man," wrote Emerson, "when duty whispers low, 'thou must' the youth replies, 'I can.'"

YOU CAN

(606)

If you think you are beaten, you are,
    If you think you dare not, you don't,
If you'd like to win, but think you can't,
    It's almost a cinch you won't.

If you think you'll lose, you're lost,
    For out in the world we find,
Success begins with a fellow's will —
    It's all in the state of mind.

If you think you're outclassed, you are,
    You've got to think high to rise.
You've got to be sure of yourself before
    You can ever win a prize.

Life's battles don't always go
    To the stronger or faster man,
But soon or late the man who wins
    Is the man WHO THINKS HE CAN!

— Selected